MEDITATION IN SIKH RELIGION

Eight Spiritual Lessons on Finding the Truth

As we develop our inner being, live more inwardly than most men do, then the balance is changed and we are pulled inwardly more by the Word of God, and a larger dream consciousness opens before us.

MEDITATION IN SIKH RELIGION

Eight Spiritual Lessons on Finding the Truth

BHAGAT SINGH THIND

New Age Books

Meditation in Sikh Religion

ISBN: 978-81-7822-344-5

First Indian Edition: Delhi, 2010

Published by
NEW AGE BOOKS
A-44 Naraina Phase-I
New Delhi-110 028 (INDIA)
Email: nab@vsnl.in
Website: www.newagebooksindia.com

Printed in India
at Shri Jainendra Press
A-45 Naraina Phase-I, New Delhi-110 028

Contents

Publisher's Note

Meditation in Sikh Religion implies that a greater whole-being, whole-knowledge, and whole-power is needed in order to weld all into a greater unity of whole-life. Each individual must have high and stric mental and moral ideals controlling and uplifting the vital and physical man in him, and no spiritual ideal liberating him from himself into his inner being.

In order to know the part, one must have the knowledge of the whole it forms a part of. The soul is larger than the ego, and large than the unconscious, the subconscious, and the superconscious.

Lying behind all phenomena is the power of God, which coordinates and correlates all into unity and synthesis; it's name is Nãm. The self-awareness of Nãm is only received by the grace and power of His Holy of Nãm, whose knowledge is vouchsafed by the gracious *guru*.

The eight lessons presented in this book by its author, Pooran Avatar Sat-Guru-Bhagat Singh Thind, to truth-seekers of the world, give guidance, truth, and wisdom to all who are ready for self-and God-realization. Dr. Thind's words stimulate and render active those powers which are normally latent, and which the seeker cannot evoke unassisted.

Editor
New Age Books

School
that is
try an
nology
culture
that w
inevita
the go
A F
ralistic
nomic
are all
tion's
The
ogies,
hunger
nation
trums
slogans
or get
too for

Vital Consciousness

In America, the development of mind is measured by its outer expressions and achievements in the objective world. Schools and universities alike seem to have only one aim, and that is of making a man fit for the purpose of economic security and power, and they are being converted into great technological institutions instead of centers of moral and spiritual culture—for the head as well as the heart and the knowledge that will bring about their synthesis and unification. This is inevitable where sense pleasures dominate and are chosen as the goal of life.

A rational and scientific formula of the vitalistic and materialistic human being and his life, a search for a perfected economic society and the democratic cultus of the average man, are all that the modern mind presents us in this, our civilization's crisis, as a light for its solution.

There is a chaos of clashing creeds, mental ideas, and idealogies, urges of individual and collective wants and needs, hungers and calls for life satisfaction of individual classes and nations, a rich fungus of political, social, and economic nostrums and notions, a maddening medley of mind-born slogans and panaceas for which men are trained to kill others or get killed to impose them on others by the immense and too formidable means of modern implements of warfare too horrible to describe—in the belief that this is the way out to something ideal.

Reason and science can only help by standardizing—by fixing everything into an artificially arranged and mechanized unity of material life. A greater whole-being, whole-knowledge, and whole-power is needed to weld all into a greater unity of whole-life.

The means science has placed at our disposal eliminate the peril of the subversion and destruction of an effete civilization by stronger primitive peoples; but it is the resurgence of the barbarian in ourselves, in the civilized man, that is the peril we see all around us. For that is bound to come, if there is no high and strenuous mental and moral ideal controlling and uplifting the vital and the physical man in us and no spiritual ideal liberating him from himself into his inner being.

The system of civilization created by man has become too big for his limited mental capacity and understanding and his still more limited spiritual and moral capacity to utilize and manage a too dangerous servant of his blundering ego and its appetites. A perfect community can exist only by the perfection of its individuals; and perfection can come only by the discovery and affirmation in life by each person of his own spiritual being and the discovery by all of their spiritual unity and a resultant life unity.

All of the outer props to which man has pinned his faith are now crumbling before his very gaze; therefore it is all the more necessary that he build an inner security, which shall be able to withstand the shocks of outer misfortunes. The true vision of the reality of his being will forbid gloom.

Psychology of the conscious mind of man cannot be adequately known without the deeper and fuller knowledge of the unconscious and subconscious background of his being—as today cannot be rightly understood without the knowledge of yesterdays which have influenced it. In order to know the part, one must have the knowledge of the whole it forms a part of. All conscious, subconscious, and unconscious activities of men's minds function purposively, and they are linked and controlled by a unifying principle and power of the innate Godhead. One state of mind cannot be properly studied without total integration of the mind. We have to go beyond the mind and reason. The reason active in our waking consciousness is only a mediator between the subconscious All, which we come from in our evolution upward—and the superconscious All, toward which we are impelled by that evolution. The subconscious and the superconscious are two different formulations of the same All. The masterword of the subconscious is life; the masterword of the superconscious is *light.*

There is something in us which is conscious when we sleep, when we are stunned or drugged or in a swoon, in all apparently unconscious states of our physical being. Our consciousness of the ego is only a small selection from our entire conscious being. It is a superficies; it is not even the whole of our mentality. Behind it, much vaster than it, there is a subliminal or subconscious mind which is the greater part of ourselves and contains heights and profundities which no man has yet measured or fathomed.

When we speak of subconscious mind, we should mean by the phrase a thing not different from the outer mentality, but only acting below the surface, unknown to the waking man in the same sense, if perhaps with a deeper plunge and a larger scope. But the phenomenon of the subliminal self far exceeds the limits of any such definition. It includes an action not only immensely superior in capacity but quite different in kind from what we know as mentality in our waking self. We therefore have a right to suppose that there is a superconscious in us, as well as a subconscious.

Are there not, in us and in the world, forms of consciousness which are sub-mental, to which we can give the name of vital and physical consciousness? There is such a vital consciousness which acts in the cells of the body and the automatic vital functions so that we go through purposeful movements and obey attractions and repulsions to which our mind is a stranger. All these are movements of consciousness but, as far as we can see, not of mentality.

His surface physical being is all that man knows, and he does not know even all of that. Below is the occult surge of his subconscious and his subliminal mind, his subconscious and subliminal life-impulses, his subconscious corporeality—all that large part of himself which he does not know and cannot govern, but which rather knows and governs him. He can only have so much power over his existence as he is identified with by self-awareness; the rest is governed by its own consciousness, which is subliminal to his surface mind and life and body.

The dream-consciousness seems to be wholly devoid of that control which the waking consciousness exercises to a certain extent over life-circumstances; it has the nature-automatism of a subconscious construction, and nothing of the conscious will and organizing force of the evolved mind of the human being. In sleep, waking activities are in abeyance, the surface mind is at rest, and normal conscious action of the bodily part of us is still. But the inner consciousness is not suspended. It enters into new inner activities, only a part of which—a part happening or recorded in something of us that is near the surface—we remember. There is maintained in sleep near the surface an obscure subconscious element which is a receptacle or passage for our dream experiences and itself also a dream-builder; but behind it is the depth and mass of the subliminal, the totality of our concealed inner being and consciousness, which is of quite another order.

This subliminal is a meeting-place of the consciousness that emerges from below by evolution and the consciousness that has descended from above for involution. There is in it an inner mind, an inner vital being of ourselves, an inner or subtle physical being larger than our outer being and nature. This inner existence is the concealed origin of almost all in our surface self.

If we develop our inner being, live more inwardly than most men do, then the balance is changed and we are pulled inwardly more by the Word of God, and a larger dream-consciousness opens before us. Our dreams can take on a subliminal and no longer subconscious character, and can assume a reality and significance.

The subliminal, with the subconscious as an annex of itself—for the subconscious is also part of the behind-the-veil entity—is the seer of inner things and of supraphysical experiences. The surface subconscious is only a transcriber. Our waking state is unaware of its connection with the subliminal being, although it receives from it—without any knowledge of the place of origin—the inspirations, institutions, ideas, will-suggestions, sense-suggestions, and urges to action that rise from below or from behind our limited surface existence.

Our mind stands between an occult subliminal existence and an outward cosmic phenomenon. It receives inspirations, intuitions, imaginations, impulsions to knowledge and action, figures of subjective realities or possibilities from the unknown inner source. It receives the figures of realized actualities and their suggestions of further possibility from the observed cosmic phenomenon.

Our mind is an observer and user of actualities, a diviner or recipient of truths not yet known or actualized, a dealer in possibilities that mediate between the truth and actuality. But it has not the omniscience of an infinite consciousness. It is limited in knowledge, and has to supplement its restricted knowledge by imagination and discovery.

The subliminal is like an urgent sea out of which the waves of our conscious becoming arise. This is the *sahaja* state, from which all becomings of the Being of God from timelessness appear in time; and the subconscious is an inferior, lowest occult province of our nature. The true subconscious is other than the vital or physical substratum; it is the unconscious vibrating in the borders of consciousness, sending up its notions to be changed into conscious stuff, swallowing into its depths impressions of past experience as seeds of unconscious habit, and returning them constantly, but often chaotically, to the surface consciousness, missioning upward much futile or perilous stuff of which the origin is obscure to us, in dream, in mechanical repetitions of all kinds, in untraceable impulses and motives in mental, vital, physical perturbations and upheavals, in dumb automatic necessities of our obscurest parts of nature.

What happens when the conscious peeps into the subconscious, or the subconscious overflows the conscious, when one enters the no-man's-land between the subliminal and the surface?

When a man explores the hidden recesses and depths of his own being, his own psyche, he finds primordial images, pictures of racial experiences, archetypes, and ancient powerful forces which have influenced his character and actions, all unseen and unknown to him. He identifies himself solely with the name and form he wears now in his present existence. He is ignorant of his past before birth, even as of his future after death. Yet all that he forgets is contained, present and effective, in the all-retaining integral consciousness within him. In his superficial consciousness he is to himself dynamically, practically, the man of the moment—not the man of the past, who once was but is no longer in existence, nor the man of the future, who is not yet in being. It is by memory that he links himself with the one by anticipation of the other.

It is the whole man who is really doing the action, and not merely this particular part of him. What he does, the way he does it, the elements he brings into it, the stamp he gives to his work, depend on his whole character, mind, information, and genius; all that the past of him has made him—and not his past in this life only, but in other lives, and again not only his past, but the past, the present, and the predestined future, of both himself and the world around him—are the determinants of his work.

All human thought, all mental man's experience, moves between constant affirmation and negation. There is for his mind no truth of idea, no result of experience that cannot be affirmed, none that cannot be negated. So, as he looks within, he believes and doubts and wonders whether he has lived before—or is it the race alone that lives, but no individual entity, and it is the race's experience, but not his?

As a tree grows by a subconscious or unconscious assimilation of action of sun and rain and wind and absorption of earth-elements, so the being grows by a subliminal or intraconscious assimilation and absorption of its results of past becoming and an output of potentialities of future becoming. The law that deprives us of the memory of past lives is a law of the cosmic wisdom and serves, not disserves, its evolutionary purpose.

When he learns through the peep into the deep of his being that his personal ego, the surface mental man, no longer dominates the scene, his personal satisfactions fade into relative insignificance and he becomes aware for the first time of the drama of ancient forces and latent life-tendencies of lives lived long ago; he awakens to know that the ego is not the center of his psyche and the king of his life.

This adventure of exploring the hidden world that lies behind man's surface ego is indeed very alluring, but full of dangers and pitfalls. Woe to the reckless adventurer who undertakes to travel without knowledge or experience or true seriousness of purpose. One who goes to the arctic or antarctic regions without due preparation, merely to escape from life's boredom or difficulties, is headed for a rude awakening and possible perdition. In just the same way, if one seeks the inner world in order to escape from reality and turns his back on the world, he too will be overwhelmed with forces he neither understands nor has the capacity to conquer and assimilate. To take up meditative science as a means of escape from life's heavy burdens is not to experience God, but rather to fall into the vast subconscious and unconscious and be swallowed up.

Subconscious and unconscious contents have an innate tendency in them to be projected to the outer world of the superficial ego, where they fasten themselves onto any willing and convenient carrier who presents a suitable peg, and exert a fascination, calling one away from reality. It becomes increasingly hard to resist them, the more a fantasy is indulged in. Reality is the great test of values; if a thing works, has a counterpart in nature, it is reality and not a dream. Soon the disillusion creeps in, the spell is broken and glamour gone, and one's last state is found to be worse than the first one. Visions and thoughts can prove themselves of value through their application in the outer world alone. If the inner fits the outer like the glove the hand, it is correct; otherwise, it was the phantasm of the subconscious.

If progress is to be made in development, then all the subconscious contents of the mind have to be brought to consciousness and assimilated or eliminated. An individual who refuses entirely to face the problem of his own amoral desires may, it is true, die in the "odor of sanctity." But that is not the end of the story. It behooves him to find some way of assimilating the evil or eliminating it from his own subconscious and unconscious life, which dominates his ego.

But if identification with good and repression of evil affect no real change of character, what further can be done? No use for a man to identify himself with the subconscious or unconscious and let the moods come as they will—now an evil one, now a good one, each following the other like the waves of the sea—while he himself takes no responsibility for their occurrence.

Is man responsible for the moods in his subconscious or unconscious? Is he directly or indirectly responsible for them? The unconscious and the subconscious are part of nature, the seat of his character, and are beyond his control. The power of conscious reasoning is a later development in the evolutionary process, playing but a minor part even in the most highly developed human being on the surface, so to speak, on the firmly built edifice of instincts, emotions, and desires, which form the main structure of mental organism. Rational conduct is not universal, for it does not employ or follow out all sides of our human nature.

Are the actual motives of human actions always instinctive, unconscious, or subconscious? What part is left for reason, that most distinctive of human powers, to play in the drama of life? What do we mean when we speak of "rational conduct" and the "rational life"? Can our reason really control conduct, and how precisely can it do so?

It is impossible to overcome natural tendencies by reason alone. Reason's reasonableness depends on its content and grasp of data. At all events, reason's sweetness, strength, and light cannot exceed the character and enlightenment of the reasoner.

Man is no more responsible for his moods and the events that confront him than the navigator is responsible for the hurricanes and tidal waves that stir the sea and toss his ship like a cork. The mariner cannot direct these, but he can direct his ship in relation to them; he can take an attitude toward them, instead of drifting with them. In the same way, the attitude which a man takes toward the moods of his unconscious or subconscious and ceaseless flow of events determines the direction he is moving in.

Man must be free from the unchecked sway of both his unconscious instincts and subconscious negations and all external codes of conduct before he can set reason free to do its work in the ethical field.

Knowledge and some small measure of control of the processes of the unconscious and the subconscious may be attained, as it were, from the surface, which represents the conscious part of the mind. Over the springs of life themselves, the most highly developed mind and the most powerful will can have no control, unless one seeks the *guru* for the knowledge of the unification of the mind and its entrance into the supra-natural sphere, where the Word abides in His fullness.

An intellectual idea, however worthy, cannot release us from the powerful forces of the unconscious and subconscious nature and the ego. The power or value which is to redeem us must have in it the power to release within us energies superior to those wielded by the conscious, the subconscious, and the unconscious sides of our lives combined.

The solution cannot be found in rational idealism, nor can it be sought in modern churches. Within our own beings, the being of supra-personal values must be found; bigger than all the hidden and manifested powers of the ego of men and all the powers of the unconscious, subconscious, and superconscious minds—the Lord of Life, ruler of the subjective as well as objective sides of life, of the within as well as the without.

Our utmost universalization on the surface is a poor and limping endeavor—it is a construction, a make-believe, and not the real thing. For in our surface consciousness we are bound to separation of consciousness from Him and from others, and we wear the fetters of the ego.

However powerful imagination or suggestion may be, they cannot give more than the mind or ego that offers them contains, nor can they change the personality by integrating the emotions.

Ego must be surpassed, the ocean of the unconscious must be crossed, only so we can take our place in the stream of life and submit ourselves to that supra-personal value which alone can give significance and dignity to the individual. The "I" itself, the ego-consciousness, is an outgrowth of the unconscious, since unconscious life exists before any trace of ego-consciousness is present. He who has outgrown his mental swaddling clothes will not fail to abandon both the geocentric view in astronomy and the egocentric theory in psychology. The soul is larger than the ego, and larger than the unconscious, the subconscious, and the superconscious.

The unconscious and the conscious, the subjective as well as the objective, are a pair of opposites; they cannot appear and disappear without something real in which they can have their risings and settings. There is a splitting up, but no division; there is a scattering of our spiritual treasures. But everywhere the soul remains entire, both in its inner sentiments and outer forms.

The true teacher instructs the true seeker in the principle of unification, which constitutes the "nextness" of representations in consciousness to one another. A spiritual principle as the agent of this act of transforming and uniting the different parts of our being is needed and is available within the being of each and all. Unity of consciousness involves a real owner, a pure spiritual entity, relation to whom makes the constituents of consciousness stick together. This agent, the Holy Name (Nām) is within and beyond each man and continuous with him, an omniscient power, most friendly to him and to his ideals, and in whom all opposites are reconciled and fulfilled.

There is the backlying power of God which coordinates and correlates all into unity and synthesis; its name is Nām. Conditioned beings put into conditioned existences can never free themselves and join the unconditioned and the uncreated God, except by the grace and power of His Holy Nām, whose knowledge is vouchsafed by the gracious *guru.*

Man can no more set himself free from the action of his instincts, which are the cause of passions and means for his growth, than he can alter the life-processes of his body, which flow from the chemical and physical constitution of the living protoplasm of which it consists.

Through the transforming and unifying powers of the Nām, one is transported into *sahaja bhava*, the state of egolessness. Here the soul is in its real nature, free and unfettered, unlimited by the ego and full of bliss, where desire cannot possibly arise. Ego is the root of discontent, desire, and the fever of possession, arch-deceiver and enemy of right knowledge; and yet this ego is the proof of the true soul or self within.

The state of egolessness is not nothingness; here the full being, the soul, is manifest, of which ego was only a fragment. He who is firmly established in the *sahaja* state will not be moved by the severest trials. Those who have not won this state through meditation and the grace of the *guru* and God react just like ordinary men to praise and blame. They are still bound to duality—the conditioned existence. They have moods; rather, moods have them. The methodology of winning this *sahaja* state must be learned from the *guru.*

The soul has to be cauterized to rid it of the infection of egoism, burning away the passion for possession, the carnal craving and the brutal reach for power. It is foolishness to seek to end the ego by the ego itself. Find its source, become united to it, and experience this unity; then the sense of separation or ego will fade away itself. Seek its source and surrender it, to be transformed by the supreme power of His *shabad*—the Word. Attainment of the *sahaja* state is true spiritual birth; then death is dead once and for all.

The happiness of deep sleep is due just to its egolessness. Imperfect and negative as it is, in deep sleep there is no body or mind or ego-consciousness, but we are as sure as we can possibly be that we ourselves survive in sleep. The source of "I am" in ego is found by the ingathering of all the vital and mental energies and directing them heartward toward the subliminal. To him who dives thus is success assured. The mysterious powers of the Holy Nām arise from within and take possession of his mind for synthesis with the heart, the subliminal.

The sojourner of the *sahaja* state is egoless, master of his mind and heart. His activity is far more efficient because of his egolessness than it would be if he willed it; his state is of utmost activity. The true *guru* pushes the disciple's mind inside from without, and pulls it in from within, and joins him to the Holy Nām and thus grants him the experience of the fullness of his soul, which will make him free. And for this work of grace to be accomplished, the disciple must practice devotion to the *guru.*

So long as an individual's action is in relation to personal and ego ends, no development of the psyche will take place. Only when a relation to a value beyond personal wishes and desires has been established can any real development and maturity result.

Relationship based upon common interest is not lasting. When the common interest ceases, the bond also ceases, and the most intimate love and devotion pass over into hatred and distrust. Only when it is based upon truth and loyalty does the bond remain so firm that it overcomes everything.

No great psychological development is possible if love and devotion to the *guru* remain on a casual or cheap level; only the single-hearted in their devotion can free themselves from such bonds as bind them to the life of mortality and suffering.

None can cross *bhava sagar*, the ocean of nature unconscious, subconscious, conscious, and even superconscious, without the knowledge of the inner path and the *guru*. The ocean of life is strewn with frail barks, which have not reached the shore of the Promised Land; some are nearly swamped, some are hopelessly shipwrecked, and others are drifting aimlessly.

If there were no *guru* and no grace, deliverance would never be possible—for the utmost efforts of finite beings can never produce infinite results. Grace is the power by which God draws the soul into Himself. Grace is the power of His Holy Nām, and its function is the lifting up of the soul by dissociating it from the sheaths. After this the real self or soul shines in its own glory and grandeur.

Akal purkh, the Ever-Enduring Being, the Perfect, is the being who in Himself and His Being has conceived and begotten all beings, without whom and apart form whom there is no true being, and in whom all things and all beings have their being. For he is the Being and background of all beings, and possesses within Himself both timelessness and time. The divided and imperfect is that which has sprung from this perfect being, just as a ray of light that goes forth from the sun and shines upon something; and it is called the creature and of all these divided beings and things, one is the perfect. Therefore also is the perfect none of the divided. When the perfect is realized, the divided is glorified and deified and surrenders itself. Thus when one gazes into his own inner being, he feels his life pulsing with him, which is the very life of God Himself, and his own life is verily just his "God's" life, and both are eternally one. The inner and the outer, the conscious and the unconscious, no longer exist for him.

We have not lost our consciousness of ourselves in God-state, but we have consciously and willingly lost or given up our short-sighted, imperfect, and egoistic self-will in the wiser and more perfect divine will, in which we cannot err. Our character and aims become identical with Him. The saint rejoices in the atmosphere of constant communion with the One who has captured the love, homage, and adventure of his soul for eternity. The presence of God in the soul is an inexhaustible fountain of inspiration to him. The soul's complete rest and satisfaction forever in God, whom the soul loves and adores and who loves the soul in return—this goal is now realized.

Every law of nature is supreme in its own realm, else it would not be a law. A magnet may take hold of objects and move them in a line directly opposite to that in which gravity acts, but this does not suspend the Newtonian law; the object yields only to the action of the stronger force affecting it for the time being. If the action of the magnet is cut off, the object yields to the pull of the earth's attraction and falls. The stronger force of the magnet acting in a contrary direction had interfered with and prevented the characteristic results of gravity. This interference of one force obeying its laws with the action of another force obeying its laws is a common and necessary phenomenon in physical nature.

There is a force which pulls the soul upward to unite it with God, from whom now it is separated, and there is a force of the earthly elements that drags it down into the meshes of mind and matter. To be detached is to be loosened from every tie that binds the soul to the earth, to be dependent on nothing temporal. Unless the personal self of man is led by forces internal to the soul itself, there is no growth of peace and joy from within; man remains earth-bound, sense-bound, and mind-bound. The object of meditation is to allow *this force from above* to work on the personal self to transform it, to fit it for being lifted up and united with the whole being within, so that egoism will be extirpated. Of what use is the sweeping away of mental cobwebs every day, when one destroys not the spider—the worldly self—that spinneth them?

Practice of Truth

THE EXTERNAL world is to man as his own mind and vision of it accords with the state of his mind and capacity of inner awareness. Nothing can be found in the external world which he does not already possess potentially or kinetically in his own mind; because the one reflects the other. Unless mind is evolved to the extent that it feels an inner surge, a rising awareness of the need of his being, it will not be affected in some way by the problem; and it will not and could not come within the mind's sphere of knowledge at all. Thus, man's inner needs of a growing soul and outer deeds and supplies are related to each other. The more he inwardly unfolds, the more outwardly he will enfold; the more he develops from within, the more he will envelope from without. Man thinks in accordance with his interests; the wider and deeper are his interests, the broader is his action. Each man's event happens according to what he inwardly is, and not otherwise.

The life of man is a double series—a series of effects produced in him by the rest of the world, and a series of effects produced in that world by him. And they are cumulative in value, building the man within and transforming the world without, or ruining the man inside and turning the world into hell outside. Each man's event does not just happen, but happens just according to what he is in inner awareness, and not otherwise. He is where he is on account of what he is. All external conditions take their color and cast from his internal quality of life and constitution. As evolution and development of the soul proceeds and progresses, each one has to reckon with the incalculable that waits for him outside. From all eternity those events and circumstances have been traveling to meet him at that particular stage of his soul's growth to deliver their messages; their shock of contact produces what it was impossible for the unaided spirit to originate alone. All events are ultimately spiritual.

To the growing soul the world is ever revealing its deeper and hidden heart of charm and beauty. The process of evolutionary development consists in changing and transforming oneself from one character to a different and distant one, a higher one, in a connected series in the scale of being, through the infilling of one's own nature by realizing finer and still finer susceptibilities. The most important thing is not what happens to oneself in life, but that in sunshine or darkness the steering of the ship of life be true.

The conscious thought of man can only reveal to him a part of any subject that engages his attention. That is why man is in a perpetual state of conscious dissatisfaction. Where only part is known, who shall say how much lies hidden?

A man's conduct cannot be understood unless we comprehend the inner springs of his actions. Behavior is not caused by his conscious mind, but by the power of the subconscious. Mere unearthing of one's hidden desires, emotions, and buried complexes, and uncovering them to be recognized is not sufficient. One must not only be able to analyze oneself, he must be able to turn a new leaf in his life and thus reconstruct his whole life by truth.

Mere knowledge of the subconscious urges and the causes

of repression cannot restore mental balance. Awakening of the sleeping mind is needed until one has aroused a deep demand in his being for truth and his mental states can operate under the erupting force of ideal from within; one cannot be ready for the integration of his personality.

When the individual's conscious self is suppressed, then the submerged life, the hinterland beyond the frontier, comes into operation and one brings to light the ancient and buried factors. The first thing demanded of him is the recognition that there is evil in his nature. Mere acknowledgment of the fact is not sufficient. Like the heroes of old who fought and slew the hydra-headed dragon, the *shesh naga* personifying the evil of their day, he also has to prepare to risk his life and limb in the fight against the monsters in the subconscious and the unconscious.

Many solutions have been suggested by many religions and schools of thought. Some get over the difficulty by declaring that there is no evil—it is only a whim or false thinking produced by our ignorance. Others declare that man is already perfect and must visualize accordingly. Others say that by giving fat offerings and donations to churches and priests, evil can be eliminated. Still others affirm that a certain savior of a certain race died for them, so all sin and evil has been annulled ever since.

The source of evil is not in Satan or Adam's apple-bite; it is our own sense of ego, placed by God in us, and its vast and varied past hidden inside of us. It may prove a boon or curse to us, according as we subject ourselves to God's will or not. It is this overweening sense of self that has grown as a barrier between God and man and keeps man wandering from sin to sin.

Seers of all times are agreed that the supreme values in life are the abstract values of truth, goodness, and beauty—ideals and principles of life. But before they can become powerful dynamics of life or motivating forces for the hearts and minds of men in general, they have to be demonstrated in concrete situations by perfected beings, whom God sends from above to show mankind His way to them. Such a personality is that of the *guru*.

It is indeed most difficult for weak man to resist evil and do good with his own powers alone; yet if he were primed with another personality possessing dynamic divine powers, he could acquire transcendental capacity for the purpose; and with the sword and support of the *guru*'s wisdom, the *guru* helps the weak man slay and win victory over the dragon infesting his subconscious and unconscious realms—which often overflow his little life of the ego. Freedom of will, combined with the *evolutionary progressive tendencies of the Divine Spirit*, by the grace of the *guru*, will overcome the overcomers in him. The strength of the knowledge of his mind and intellect will never accomplish the task alone.

The outward world has its own kind and degree of reality, but it is not real in its own right. In like manner, the inner world has its own kind and degree of reality, but it is not real in its own right. The outward world is real, and so is the inner world real, but only as an aspect of God, which is *One*.

There is undoubtedly a remarkable "fit" between the inward and outward minds and world. It is like the fit of the glove to the hand, or like two blades to a pair of scissors. The outward and inward are certainly not divided by an absolute chasm; they are like husband and wife, like Shakespeare's lovers, "Two distincts and diversion none." The bridge between them, unifying them, is known; and the method of crossing is verifiable by each and all who seek life's fullness and wholeness. It is a supra-rational way of passing beyond the upper end of the highest round of our mental ladder; we must leave the ladder and cross the "bridge," the narrow path that leads to life, through the power of the Holy Name (Nām) by the grace of the *guru.*

Without the *guru,* the guide, the way is not found and men are lost in the wide wilderness of the subconscious. When the intelligent conscious life of the person is suppressed, there is a distinct drop in the worth of the communication which results; it lacks the mature wisdom, the selective insight, and the balance of judgment of the integrated and unified mind. When the whole being is unified, with all the powers of the mind working harmoniously, the effect is infinitely richer than when the subconscious life automatically presents its product ready made to the passive mind. A lunatic is an individual completely overcome by the subconscious or the unconscious.

Emotions are not "made" or wilfully produced in and by consciousness. Instead, they appear suddenly, leaping up from an unconscious region. We are repeatedly surprised afresh to discover that, in spite of us, something can jump upon our back or fall upon our head out of mere nothingness, radically altering the pattern of our individual or social life.

What is actually happening in the world is due not entirely to "dim remnants of formerly conscious activities," but to volcanic outbursts of the bottom of the unconscious realm in us. No lofty well-grown tree ever disowned its dark roots. In fact, it grows not only upward but downward as well. By the powers of the divine Word, all this is changed and absorbed by man as an asset in the elevation of his soul's sovereignty. The Holy Name changes common matter into noble by tinting it into a glorious color (*lal rung*); *its dye-stuff ennobles ignoble substances.*

All work done under the immediate direction of attention is slow, inaccurate, and exhausting. To will from the brain is extremely fatiguing and invariably leads to physical and mental breakdown. The brain and mind use up energy, while the sympathetic system increases it. Functional ailments are produced by mental conflicts and frustration; yet the struggling person finds himself utterly helpless to overcome them, in spite of self-analysis and psychoanalysis. Psychotherapy brings relief temporarily, but it cannot give sufficient strength and stamina to the mind.

The way to the Word within—the Holy Name—is long, and how to make a start on that way is what most men need to be taught. The science of astronomy opens the door to the marvels of the outer world, and the science of meditation opens the door to the wonders of the inner world. The distance between any two points in the inner realm may be as incalculable as the distance between any two points in the outer realm. The only way of understanding and realizing the immense distances between mental and spiritual states is to compare them with the immense distances in the external universe. The western nations suffer from total absence of such classification, which is responsible for the chaotic condition of the inner world today.

To know God as the Being of my being, the Soul of my soul; to enter one's own being in His Being, to know this truth, to experience it not as a theory, not as a conclusion or conviction, not as a poetic idea, not as a hidden sudden revelation, but as the central fact of one's own inmost life; by being established in Him, by living it, by being it, is the final end of all spiritual effort.

God is beyond my outward form, beyond my physical sensations, beyond perception, beyond conscious thought, beyond emotions and feelings of the heart, beyond all the constituent elements of my selfhood. And all these must be transcended, and the things that belong to them or are associated with them must cease to be desired for their own sake if the self of man and Self of God are to meet.

The ignoble conception of being saved by a minimum of personal effort in the form of mechanical obedience to authoritative direction finds no sanction or countenance in these teachings.

When Nām—the Holy Word—is given or taken as the unifying factor, the integrating element, all mental states inconscious, unconscious, subconscious, conscious, and superconscious, are gathered together, brought into harmonized already inwardly existing unity amongst themselves. The integrated, fully synthesized being operates for the good and happiness of all, naturally and entirely.

The superconscious or *sahaja* state can be attained only when the whole being is unified. A unified mind has tremendous healing and renewing influence on the body. The strength of such unified personalities lies in their fourth-dimensional experience; they are surcharged with the divine energies and become mighty magnets of truth, goodness, and beauty. They do not utter a single word—they do not live, so their words usher in a new age, a new civilization. Transforming power is in their very integrated personalities, radiating, like the sun, the inner attributes of their Godhead.

If we concentrate the mind on material articles, particles, or entities we can gain the power of concentration, no doubt; but its effects are dangerous, debilitating, and destructive to the concentrator. The ego of man cannot be lifted up beyond the time-space relationship by concentrating on things that themselves constitute a part of time-space relationship. It is impossible to fix the mind, which is extremely restless, on external symbols—which have no power to give calm and peace to it, nor have they the capacity to destroy its dirt. Such external concentration can never change the inner nature of the seeker; not even omnipotence approaching from without could bring about other action from bee, bird, beast, or man, except what is constitutional to each. The Holy Spirit of Nām is not of the conscious individual; it is of the universal, between which and the individual a connection most vital is never severed. The word of God alone regenerates and transforms the being from within. Hence, concentration of the Nām, which is purity incarnate, the living fountain of the Holy Nām, casts out everything effete and impure and refreshes the soul with new sources of inspiration and wealth, restoring its original sweetness, expression, and force. It delivers it from the bondage of its former transgressions.

When the concentration is very deep and the mind does not waver, but remains focused and poised, pulled by the power of the Nām inward against all pulls of an earthly nature, ready to sink into its source, then at such a moment a mysterious power of the Holy Name rises from the inmost core of one's being and takes complete possession of one's mind and life and ushers it into *sahaja bhava*, the egoless state.

Meditation is not merely a nice thought, a poetic flight, loose fancies, or psychic surge or stir, or even pleasant experiences. It is a depth of concentration in which the mind flows continuously toward its center of fixity without any cessation, as "oil poured from one vessel to another." "Life" is the name given to it.

A change of heart seems a trifling circumstance, but it implies a change of the entire man and his whole life. If you wish to conquer the ills of life and death and triumph over them, then invocation and meditation on the Holy Nām is the only problem-solver of the soul. Man is a "cluster," a composite entity. Nām is the only unifying power and principle of his divine author within. He who is joined to Nām—the

Holy Word—is inseparably one in his form with the form of the Lord God of the universe.

The view that a man's best convictions spring from concurrence of all sides of his nature, inconscious, unconscious, subconscious, conscious, and superconscious, is supported by the prevalent fruitful conceptions of organism. A living organism is that in which every functional part works in coordination with the whole and may adjust itself in compensatory mode to the excessive or deficient action of other parts. The best state is when everything functions in coordination with the rest. Such unification and harmonization is realized in meditation alone, where the whole being is united for fullest living and expression in God's holy presence and oneness.

When all that is without has flowed into the within; when the opposition between I and world, without and within, nature and spirit, has disappeared, man knows his own self and his God's to be identically one Self, one Being. This is realization.

Some advise the student to make the mind blank, a vacuum, by eliminating or controlling all thoughts that try to rise. There is a danger in this form of practice in the beginning, especially to those who are not mentally and morally strong; they may easily enter into a negative and passive state, and it is in such states the subconscious contents become operative—because all controls and censorship of the conscious are withdrawn. Some of the modern cults and groups say they can hear the voice of God and receive directions from Him by keeping the mind a vacuum. It is very rash and risky to depend on such experiences as being valid, because whoever goes to himself risks a confrontation with his past "self or selves." The mirror does not flatter; it faithfully shows whatever looks into it—namely, the face we never show to the world, because we cover it with the mask, the mask of the actor. But the mirror lies behind the mask and shows the true face.

To let the unconscious or the subconscious happen and to experience it as a reality is risky. It exceeds the courage as well as power of an average person who is weak in spirit. The figures that appear are fairies or beguiling sirens and *lamias*, who infatuate the lonely wanderer and lead him astray. Hallucinatory or visionary perceptions take place that can be nothing else than the projection of the unconscious and the subconscious. Here, either consciousness is completely inundated with childishness, or it must constantly defend itself, or advancing into the unconscious regions of the psyche it is overpowered by the archaic forces of the subconscious and finds itself in a dangerous situation, for it seems as though it were extinguishing itself as if being devoured by the Dragon of Darkness. The lowest and the highest, the best and the most atrocious, the truest and the falsest are mingled together in the unconscious, which thus opens an abyss of confusion, deception, and despair.

Concentration upon the center, the place of creative transformation, the cosmic source of energy, is most essential. Processes of purification always take place at the hallowed spots (*tirthas*), where a bath of renewal in the source of life strengthens the soul. Higher than that which is thus changed stands the Holy Nām—the Word of God—which effects change for the better. It acts like a magnet upon the disparate materials and processes of the unconscious and the subconscious and, like a crystal grating, catches them one by one and dissolves them. It is a baptismal fountain where all karmic stains in the subconscious and the unconscious are washed away. Dissolution of all karmic taints is necessary ere they attain to cosmic character; thus are the unconscious and the subconscious depotentialized, and thus diving under what is below is linked to what is above; separation of consciousness from the unconscious and the subconscious is annulled, and the reunion of the individual ego is brought about with the divine fullness of His Being in each and all.

The coalescence of the conscious, the subconscious, and the unconscious can succeed only a step at a time when the right formula for the conscious, subconscious, and unconscious correlation is learned from the gracious *guru* and practised faithfully under his guidance. The subconscious must always be first purged, purified, and cauterized, and its contents disposed of by the fire of the Holy Name; otherwise the entrance to the collective unconscious cannot be opened.

Ego-consciousness does not swallow the unconscious, nor does it repress it; it is dangerous to do so, for the unconscious is life reaching upward and full of the issues of life. If life is repressed, it will live against one. The conscious and the unconscious—both are aspects of one life. They are merged into a distinct and unique indivisible totality. Totality exceeds both ego plus non-ego.

The center of transcendental consciousness cannot be the human ego, since the ego has neither a hand in producing such experiences, nor the necessary intelligence to understand them. It can only be their victim or the receiver of divine grace. When the waves of the conscious and unconscious seas roll over the ego, he forgets who he was and does things in which he no longer recognizes himself—thus he becomes their victim. Who can still the stormy seas and calm the cyclones as they rage and rush in the conscious and the unconscious except the Word of the God, who is both the author of the unconscious and the conscious, in them and above them.

When the night comes, the light of consciousness in sleep is not extinguished but withdrawn, and the dark sea of the unconscious bursts in dream life. Here consciousness at least temporarily becomes the object of the unconscious and witnesses the scenes passively. From this arises the certainty that consciousness can also be drawn into the archetypal unity of the supraconscious, where the ego knows itself to be one with the whole being and looses its egoism and is liberated.

The state of the soul in deep sleep is that of freedom from all pains and pleasures—a negative state, but very essential in life. The loss of sleep is accounted a grievous evil; for its sake men are willing to poison the very source of life, the brain, with deadly drugs and dope. All this shows how much we love sleep, and we love it because in it we are happy—because in *sushupati* (deep sleep state) there is no ego, but only in waking and dreaming. In both of these states the ego manifests by taking hold of the body. Real self is the source of ego, and only in meditation, through the grace of the *guru,* is sought and found and fullness of life entered into. *Sahaja* state of egolessness is not in relativity.

> "There is a soul above the soul of each
> A mightier soul which yet to each belongs."

"There is a world-sea which rolls through the hearts of all and which each calls his own, while it is an all-animating pulse-beat of the whole human race."

The universal, the unconscious, precedes the individual, gives the individual its field to grow and develop cosmically, though the universal is not the home of the soul, but God—the Transcendental Being. The soul lives here by the grace of God and depends upon it. God does not exist by the individual or depend upon it. As ego is the center of consciousness, God is not only the center, but also the circumference that encloses the conscious and the unconscious. It is the center of this totality; knowledge of this total self is salvation.

The unconscious is the mother of the conscious. Where there is a mother, there should also be a father, but he seems to be unknown until one is reborn of the "water and the spirit." The conscious self—the ego, the frail youngster—may deny his father, but he cannot deny his mother. As a human mother can only produce a child potentially human, whose nature was concealed in her during gestation, so we are forced to believe that the unconscious, the universal, cannot be an altogether chaotic accumulation of instincts and images. It is not the region of darkness alone, and it is not empty. It is the "lavishing mother," the holder of His images—the seeds of all beings and their becomings. When the subconscious has been cleared, then from the depths of the unconscious, the universal "issues of life" spring forth in their glory. Some power must hold it together. Its center cannot be the ego, since the ego was born in the womb of the unconscious, the universal, through evolutionary growth, though it came from the father and turns its back on him, seeking to deny him as best it can.

If the egos, the splinters, have personality then the block, the Godhead, from which they were separated before the "world" began, must have personality to a still higher degree. The conclusion seems logical; why then should not the whole have personality, too? This personality is completely concealed and inaccessible being to all who are not born of the Word of God, the Holy Nām, and have their inner vision developed; for "only the pure in heart can see Him."

The ship of the Holy Nām is the vehicle that carries the ego through the unconscious sea of his mother and its deeper depths to the home of his father, who has waited ages to welcome home his son and heir—the only begotten one.

Great liberating deeds of world history have come from spirit-born personalities, and never from the inert mass of the common rank and file of humanity. That is secondary at all times and needs the priest and the demagogue if it is to move at all. The people always long for a hero, the slayer of the Dragon of Darkness, when it feels the danger of psychic and subtle forces; hence the cry for personality of the living liberated man—teacher of the souls, the lord-liberator, the living Word made concrete in personality—the *sat-guru.* All who seek to know the divinity within must keep company with the loftiest souls of the earth; without such *sat-sang*, or association with the elect of mankind, the deeper nature of man is not roused and made dynamic.

> "The tidal wave of deeper souls
> Into our inmost being rolls
> And lifts us unawares
> Out of all meaner cares."

The deep, strong current of peace and joy flowing in harmony with God in their inner natures soon saturates, suffuses, and softens our hard and flinty subconscious nature and induces and produces in the true seeker a true desire to welcome with delight the knowledge of the inner path to him who proves himself worthy of walking on that razor-like path within. The crust must be crushed before the waters of life shall gush forth; the comb must be broken ere the honey shall exude; the grape must be pressed before the wine shall flow forth. The alien land between the outer and the inner minds must be explored; oneness of the objectivity and subjectivity must be realized before the consciousness can be unified and made single in intent, ere the light of the living Lord shall shine in the ego and join with Him as one light. The ego is made clean by wisdom's fire from within; the crush is shattered, and the inside of man is made impervious to dirt from without. Separation is no more; no veil stands between the soul and the oversoul, between the *jiva* and the *atma.* They are now one, and *jiva* makes the *atma*—the most high—his abiding habitation and no longer seeks occasional refuge, as he did before. He is no longer helped but renewed, not revived but strongly sustained; he no longer sees the things of the spirit with the eyes of the flesh, but the things of the flesh with the eyes of the spirit; and all is peace within and without; for he has found God, and he who finds God becomes wholly God, and unto God there is no other God; they are one inseparably.

What makes the mind vigorous, powerful, and penetrating? Practice of truth and love in service in our daily tasks and practice of meditation. What converts the soft and flabby flesh into strong sinew and muscle? Practice. How does a character become strong and spiritual, grand and heroic? By practice, the bonds of heart are to be broken. As long as heart preserves desires, the mind will nourish illusions. On the path of ascent desires become stumbling blocks; they were stepping stones on the path of descent. Unless man renounces all separate desires and works with the will of the Supreme Being, his miseries will multiply thick and fast.

Divine Love

OUR MINDS, like our bodies, have developed primarily in practical relation to the external world, and we cannot possibly escape from or cope with and conquer the conditions thus imposed upon us by ourselves alone, except by the help of the powers that be, who placed us here.

We are interwoven with the sense-world and the laws of nature by which that sense-world is ruled. We are ourselves a product of this world; hence we can neither free ourselves from our separateness, nor purify ourselves from the stains we gather by coming into contact with it, nor freely and fully protect ourselves from the blows it ministers to our incipient souls without willing. Something that happens outside of us must cause something to happen inside of us. The whole universe is for us, and all the events and circumstances are for us; all things are for us; they have something to tell us, because all things have a meaning which God has placed in them for us to learn by relating them to us, by facing them, or by being forced upon them or they upon us.

We want to know how to bend this world to our wills or, as the next best thing, how to adjust ourselves to the world, so that we may be able to make the best of the world. There is the burden of all this weary, unintelligible world; we dare not deny it. We see it waiting for every man at his appointed hour. But who has tied it upon our backs forever as a thing from which seemingly there is no escape? Who has brought to pass that the weary weight never leaves us?

Opposite our window we see a rose bush. One of the thinkers, or a cult, informs us that the rose bush is "a construction of the mind." Another, that it is a "group of sense impressions," and another that it is "a projected idea." Still another says that it is "an illusion of mind and *maya*." Now, if any such interpretations of the rose bush are true, it seems certain that the rose bush is playing us a trick. We take the rose bush for just what it declares itself to be.

Are we not right in supposing that a thing can manifest itself only by coming in its true colors? If it comes out in false colors and shows itself as something other than it is, then the proper name for the process is not manifestation but masquerading or, pardon our plain language, lying.

In what ways is man's within related to world's without, and vice-versa? And how must he rightly relate himself to it? Has the world on its own part an answering "attitude" toward the enquiring mind, analogous to that of a person who has a meaning to impart to others and is taking the necessary steps to get this meaning recognized?

No object can stand before the bar of thought and maintain the character of an unknowable. Were it not for our perceptions, the outer world would not exist for us, which is very far from saying that it has no existence of its own. What is a fact for man depends upon his apprehending faculties. Were the object unknowable, thought could not apprehend it. The worth of things and our powers of recognizing and explaining them or accounting for their existence are dependent on the unfoldment and growth of the soul; that for which the capacity and susceptibility is not developed within cannot be recognized, explained, or appropriated from without for the enrichment of personality.

The abilities or energies of any people have much to do with the effects upon them of outer environments, foreign peoples or civilizations, and circumstances. What is stimulus and education for one may injure another. Some primitive tribes have gained little except disease, depression, and death from contact with civilization. Why go to history to discover truth? The degree of truth in history is the same as the degree of truth in the historian.

The habitual flow of the mind is toward the world without, not toward the world within. Even if one succeeds in turning the mind away from the world and concentrating it on the self, it breaks loose and wanders back to the world. Why has the world such a hold on us, and who has put this *maya-moha*—the love of the world—in us, and for what purpose?

Can thoughts regarding realities that confront us from within be denied admittance by a mere fiat of our wills? Also, can anyone question the reality of his inner self within? If he did, he would at once put himself out of court to be able to raise any question at all, and must admit that he exists. Which of these two worlds is real—the world without of environments and ceaseless happenings, or the world of the archetypal ideals and the self within? Are we not most of the time desiring to get hold of something from without or to get rid of something from within, and are we not most of the time unhappy?

In the world without, all things ceaselessly flow; and in the world within, are we not continuously being strengthened or weakened by what we experience without? Thus we find weight is given to the qualities of flux and abidingness at the same time. Thus two orders of recognizable or consciously active experiences work constantly upon each other. The direct apprehending of facts affects the growth and form of our thoughts and principles, while our principles and thoughts affect each fresher apprehension of facts and act more on the world of facts. By the overcoming of facts, values are gained and life made richer. Thus a continuum, a union, indeed is maintained between our past and our present, between what we were and what we are and are somewhat emergently becoming.

Is it not the world, with its vast riches in the form of experience free of access to all who could use it, quickened by the sense of growing life from within, which demands not to be explained only, but to be enriched by every contribution which experience can pour into our bosoms? Should we not open our inner eyes to see and our arms to receive whatever gifts are held in store for us by the inexhaustible riches of God and His universe, manifested for the growth of souls?

Some call the world a system, soul's nursery, a training place for humanity, an organism, a school, a workshop, a battlefield, a mine, a scene, a background, a phantasm, a lie, a myth, an illusion, or even a cemetery, a penitentiary. We do know they are all true; as we are, so is our world. Immersed as we are in the atmosphere of this limited and temporary purpose, we want no other view, and can't have it. But the advancing soul for richer experiences bursts and overflows every logical dam by which intellect seeks to confine it. Experience is always new, and our metaphysical bottles are always old. Let each one live his own life, and die his own death—suffer as well as enjoy. There are native human rights, and no one may with impunity shield another from them. Let each one learn to stand by and not interfere. Each step forward in experience—in consciousness—makes a further advance inevitable, until he has learned to sanctify every relationship. Then problem-solving will cease to be the central business of the mind, and glorification will begin, with a search for the permanent amid the changing. And Holy Nām, the Living Word, is the only form of the Eternal Being in which the permanent stands permanently expressed.

If nature produces all things, we cannot escape the conclusion that our theories of their production are themselves natural products. How can we free ourselves from nature's bond and bondage and become her masters and not remain slaves? We ask the philosopher, who explains how all things come in, not to forget to explain how he happens to come in himself and what in the total production is the significance of his part. The idea of outwitting nature at her game is extremely popular and thoroughly characteristic of this industrial age. How can one "make" anything of that whose final nature one does not understand?

Things are as they are; new names do not alter them. Evil is evil, pain is pain, death is death, and it is only in accepting them in their naked reality that religion can be true to itself. Let the gloom thicken, and her radiance then will glow like the noonday.

The cosmos is like a symphony of rarest beauty, perfect in every note, arrangement, and composition; it has a natural basis created by God for the soul's advancement, happiness, and delight. For God to subject Himself to illusion of the reality of things is a most unlikely and God-dishonoring supposition, more especially considering that He is represented as Perfect Wisdom and, therefore, must be free from all illusion and ignorance.

The real existence of the world and the soul are related to the one great whole, whose source, Nām—the Holy Word—is when the subjective and the objective existences are joined in an everlasting bond of union. In it all conflict of the within and the without forever cease. Here man is one with God in his character, one in thought, will, and desire. The true union of soul and God means that by this humanity comes to participate in God's nature; it attains to the fullest life, most personal and most intense. It is a union which means the reciprocal embrace of conscious *prem*—love divine—realized and enjoyed. God is to be worshipped by sanctifying all human pleasures to His service.

God's very character is infinite love. True love cannot rest content to live a life of self-contemplation or self-communion only. Love requires an object upon which to bestow its wealth of infinite tenderness and affection, for whom to make sacrifices, with whom to have a divine conscious, delightful communion, and fellowship. This is the highest bliss, life in its highest form, where life and love blend and become one. Creation of the world is the result of divine love, seeking object and expression.

God has not left "objective existence" to shift for itself. His is the immanent presence sharing the struggles and victories of His creatures in His cosmos dwelling in the soul of man, not as a usurper, but as a co-worker, as the Loving Father, dwelling together with His sons in the same sanctuary of the heart, bestowing upon the soul the gifts and graces which beautify and ennoble its great destiny. He reveals Himself to the soul as an ever-enduring person, as the supra-personal spiritual being.

He nourishes His sons with the nectar of His Holy Nām—the soul-strengthening substance—which He pours from above into the souls of those who meditate and move nearer to His abode in them. To the weak His Holy Name is invigorating, to the depressed a delight dispenser; it clothes each with a mantle protecting against every desolating wind of the world. Its exhilarating influence on the brain and soothing effects on the nerves and mind is unparalleled; it has medicinal properties, healing the hearts, minds, and bodies of all who partake of it. It bestows long life and wards off old age and decrepitude, and diminution of vitality is never felt by those who daily renew themselves in this bath of bliss and light. It stimulates the voice and induces singing, awakens bright thoughts and fires the being with the ever-new zest of glorious self-assertion. It girds the soul with the strength that fears no enemies and brooks no defeat. Daily nourished by this *amrita*—the nectar of immortality—the devout soul finds its life and joy in spontaneous outpourings of the heart, in loving service, in brave struggles, in fearless trust and strong illumined faith, in the kindred reciprocal love of the Supreme Father. Communion is this nearest and dearest fellowship and friendship with the indwelling lover of souls—our own God—the giver of all gifts, "guts," and victory.

The sense of power, dependent on no temporal suffrage, rings out in every one of his cries; the attitude of self-defense is foreign to his spirit who drinks deeply from this source of all strength. He must always attack, must always be of good cheer, must always go forth conquering and to conquer. His is not the half-hearted religion which negotiates for its status and proposes a perpetual parley with doubt, dearth, disease, and death. Why should not the world despise a "religion" which is accompanied by an everlasting excuse for its existence?

To meet the problems of life one must draw soul-strength from God in daily meditations to make his whole being incorruptible, to have and hold steadfast courage, inner fearlessness, and fortification that will render him invulnerable to the shocks and stabs of earthly existence. Those who seek to triumph in the struggle of life need to be nourished on ambrosia, the nectar of the Nām, the only food for the soul.

Only in and through the Nām—the Word—is the God-imminent, the only complete personality to whom the human heart can turn in all its joys and sorrows, to be realized.

It is the individual who is the "dynamic force" to regenerate humanity. It is the case always and everywhere. Individualism should therefore be prized and nourished as against "despotism," whether in church or state, at home or abroad.

The annals of humanity do not disclose anything so lofty in its teachings, so pure in its spirit, so rich in its lessons of character, sacrifice, forgiveness, and love as the examples of our worshipful *gurus, avatars,* and *mahatmas* who achieved completion of their individualities. The achievement of personality is nothing less than the best possible development of all that lies in a particular single being. It is impossible to foresee what an infinite number of conditions must be fulfilled to bring this about. Personality can never be developed unless the individual chooses his own way consciously and with conscious moral decision and is loyal to the law of his own being and is addressed only by the voice of his true and divine self—his inner man. Only completed personality acts upon society to alleviate, liberate, transform, and heal. Only the man who is able consciously to affirm the powers of his Godhead in all things confronting him from within becomes a true individual who consciously translates into his own individual reality what would lead only to ruin if it were lived unconsciously by the multitudes.

The gigantic catastrophes that threaten us are not elemental happenings of a physical or biological kind, but are psychic events. We are threatened in a fearful way by wars and revolutions that are nothing other than psychic epidemics. Psychic life is a world power that exceeds by many times all the powers of the earth.

True sons of God are the blossoms and fruits of the tree of

humanity, the seeds that continue to engender. For what, except gods, could counterbalance the dead weight of the whole of mankind and eternal habits? How hard a thing it is to control the present with all the forces of the past marching down upon us. They alone can show us the bridge that leads across the cosmic aspect and life of liberation and bliss; otherwise we remain caught up like flies in a spider's web.

Knowledge of the *shabad*—the way of the Word—is man's indispensable guide on pathless and trackless oceans of the unconscious. Through the *shabad* alone the unconscious psyche is joined to the conscious and consciousness as a co-existent entity. Life has grown dry and restricted and therefore demands the discovery of its source. But the source cannot be found unless consciousness or ego resigns itself to a return to the land of its childhood, in order to receive there, as before, guidance from the unconscious, the universal—its nurse and mother.

Only a unified personality can experience divine life; a being split up into partial aspects, though it calls itself a human being, cannot do so. Intellectual understanding, as the highest form of understanding and insight, is inferior to direct experience. To be convinced, one needs to have the experience of this unification.

Ere illumination dawns, the dragon of darkness must be slain; the inner voice must be faced, and the dragon fears the sunlight. *Gagan-mandal*, the galaxy of the inner sun, is the well-spring of life, and final wholeness of man must become dynamic and active. The problems of the inner voice are full of hidden pits and snares. It is a most dangerous and slippery region. The inner voice brings to consciousness whatever is evil in a temptingly convincing way, so as to make us succumb to it. It brings to us something not good, but evil. This must be so for the reason that we are generally not as unconscious of our virtues as of our vices, and then because we suffer less from the good than from the bad. If we do not succumb to it in part and do not allow ourselves to be suppressed by it, but are able to assimilate it, then nothing of this apparent evil goes into us; then the deeper voice of our fuller life, of a wider and more comprehensive consciousness, brings about a new renewal and new healing, and by its potently transformative tincture of the Holy Nām—the creative Word of God—brings about their complete assimilation. Without this purifying process of the Holy Name, the soul cannot rise "transfigured of all, blemish free."

However, all evil remains submerged as long as the consciousness does not come upon the scene in meditative progress. The contradictions of the subconscious and the unconscious remain latent; they cannot be depotentialized. The soul chases around the central sound of the Holy Name like a shy animal, fascinated and frightened at the same time, always running away and yet always approaching. The birth of the real person in us has a restorative effect upon the individual. It is as if a stream that was losing itself in marshy tributaries suddenly discovered its proper bed, or as if a stone that lay upon a germinating seed were lifted away so that the sprout could begin its natural growth. All the usual little remedies and medicaments of psychology and theology fall a whole lot short of this fullest connection with our source of being.

To be in *sahaja* state means fulfillment, wholeness, complete realization of existence. To be complete is to be the real person, everlasting and eternal. Development of personality is synonymous with an increase of awareness, which is characterized by addition of spiritual attributes and manifestation of life in greater abundance, and the moment of this birth of more light is unification, which brings illumination. The evolutionary stress of the spirit and its progressive tendencies moves all nature only through coercion. Working through causal connections forces human nature to move forward. Nothing changes itself without need, and human personality least of all. It is immensely conservative, not to say inert and tamasic. Only the sharpest need is able to rouse it. The development of personality obeys no wish, no command, and no insight as far as the masses are concerned, but only need. It wants the motivating coercion of inner or outer necessities. Thus the inner and the outer worlds are means for its growth. Man's ego is the iron, the inner world the anvil, and the outer world the sledgehammer. The suffering iron between them is, in the end, shaped into an unbreakable whole, the perfected individual.

The "whole" must needs include, besides consciousness, the field of unconscious events, and must constitute a sum total embracing and transcending both. The ego, once the "monarch" of this totality, is dethroned and now remains merely the center of consciousness. A whole cosmically complete lifespan in all its biological, anthropological, neurological, psychological, social, moral, and spiritual aspects is needed. Personality is the highest realization of the inborn distinctiveness of the particular living being. It is an act of greatest courage in the face of life, and means unconditional affirmation of all that constitutes the individual, the most successful adaptation to the universal conditions of human existence with the greatest possible freedom of personal decision. Hence the perfected man is the legitimate product of the laws of reincarnation and *karma* and the transformative powers of God's Holy Word, which immunizes him against all earthly pollutions and makes him impervious to all external bondage—and thus bestows upon him sovereignty of the three worlds.

As true color decoration appears in the skin of the fruit when in its inside the core of its life is filled with ripe, sweet juice, so the very nectar of His Holy Name, when imbibed by the seeker's soul, intoxicates his entire being and gives cosmic color to all of his desires and deeds. The separated, isolated life of man is like a bitter sprig which is grafted into the tree of life by the Word of God, and once grafted through initiation by the True Living Savior, the sweet juice of the tree of truth flows without interruption through the once-bitter sprig and deeply sweetens it and completely transforms it into its own likeness. Just as the outer visible sun has the power to dry up the swamps and marshes of the lowlands and destroy their impurities that breed pestilence, so has man the sun of His wisdom shining in his heart, whose spiritual sunlight smothers, suffocates, and smashes to shreds all evil influences that arise from higher psychic or astral planes within and without man.

No one can ever by means of his self-will alone overcome his own self-will and the gravitation and pull of earthly desires. Seated in lower self, in *maya* or not-self, the soul is incapable of loosening itself from them unless the gracious *guru* shows him the path to the Word within and cuts the fetters that fasten his soul to the not-self, the nature. As a sour or bitter unripe apple, by ripening in the sun, becomes changed and is sweet and juicy and agreeable in taste, but still retains the qualities that make it an apple, likewise the soul of man, born by the Word of God, retains its own essential qualities, but they are now metamorphosed and manifested in the sweetest and serenest expression of its Godhead. In not-self or nature, there is darkness. If the soul can be lifted beyond the not-self, it shall know itself to be one with God. Beyond *maya* or nature there is no darkness because there is nothing that can produce it; only the not-self veils the self; the self is ever self-effulgent.

All visible and invisible nature exists in the Divine Spirit, the visible in the outer and the invisible in the interior divine nature of God. When the Word of God enters the seeking soul, the soul is rendered pure and immaculate. No soul can become divine or deified by contemplating God as if He were something foreign to herself. God must become substantial and corporified in her; germs of evil must be torn out of the heart, or there is no wholeness of the man and no realization of God and no final safety or sanctuary.

The mere idealist is satisfied temporarily with enjoying in his mobile imagination the beauty of the ideal projected by his subjective nature, and the "realist," so called, is satisfied for a while with what he believes is real. They both live in the world of halves and in illusions. The unification of man must precede his illumination. And no man can join himself together and make himself one by his own personal powers. Only the power and presence of *sat-guru*, the savior, is capable of doing this for him. Let him entirely throw himself at the feet of him who knows Him within himself and can guide the student successfully toward the union of himself with his God-self. Let the student for a while draw the sap of the savior within from his own tree of life and become strong for the journey within. Let him possess the peace that nothing external can perturb, attain a tranquillity that no creature or circumstance can disturb; then all that God the Father is, and all that is in Him, will appear within him as soon as he is firmly focused in the spiritual region of *trikuti*, the "third heaven" within him, by the grace of the living-liberated *sat-guru*, the way-shower—the joiner of souls with God.

When the lion gets very hungry, he awakens the forest with his royal roars, and unerringly, unfailingly seeks out his prey. So does man seek the living savior when his whole being is consecrated and dedicated with an all-absorbing passion for truth and God, and he who seeks Him most surely will be shown how to find him within the interior depths of his own being. The true *guru* leads man to his God and Father within.

Without the power of the Holy Nām and its purging processes, the "Augean stable" of the self can never be thoroughly cleansed, no matter how great and grand might be the efforts. Only the Nām can invest the soul with the wonder-winged and heavenly beauty which the glorious God within has for each and all and can hush the rush of intellect, hold the wild will captive, remove the dryness of heart and breathe upon the soul the breath of His bliss and gather together the scattered self and make it whole. Nām alone can shatter the crust of alien life within—hardened, verdureless, making living barren and fruitless—and water the desert of man's heart and turn it into a valley of paradise. Only He can give him freedom from the bonds of nature, whose Word and will were instrumental in confining him therein. Freeing power is His whose Word creates, and not man's.

One must raise the focus of the self from the plane of heterogeneity to that of homogeneity and let the Holy Word pervade his being and homogenize it thoroughly before it can ascend to the cherished height of *gagan-mandal* or Mount of Transfiguration, where oneness of mind reigns over all; where the human and divine minds coalesce and combine as they were before separation took place and the path of descent began.

This marriage of minds, this conjunction and commingling, is most patently fruitful and profitable for the individual; the interchange of their essences is most regenerating and bestowing of real vitality; it is the beginning of masterful possession of a divine substance that heals and harmonizes; it is the true medicine for the healing of minds and hearts, the "elixir of life," the tincture of the Holy Name, the incorruptible force which purifies and perfects everything it passes through. It has power over thoughts and things; both are its creations. True mastery of the not-self, *maya*, nature, begins here. Man becomes a victor and ceases to be a drifter; he has now the power to lay down all thoughts, as a workman will lay down his tools and take them up again when he needs them.

There is no staying ground here yet. Whenever one reaches a comparatively still place and thinks now he has a rest, very soon something comes along that takes the wind off his sails and disturbs him and makes him uneasy. The skiff of his soul is caught in the whirlpool within, where two conflicting seas, the sea of self and the sea of God, meet. The earthly pulls are at their worst. Buffeted by these waves in this whirl of earthly and heavenly life, the *sat-guru*—the ferryman of humanity—alone can take him across the surging seas on the ship of the Holy Nām. Without the *guru*, all are drowned here; only the ship of His Word has the power to go through all hurricanes of the ocean of life.

Life, like the pendulum of a clock, swings between two poles—the pole of desire unsatisfied, unsublimated, which is pain and frustration, and the pole of desire satisfied, which is ennui. The more one looks forward to anything, the less satisfaction one finds in it when it comes. In continual becoming, without ever being, in ceaseless wishing and never feeling satisfied, there is neither peace nor joy. There is no inspiration in endless change, but there is inspiration in endless progress, and progress is when one approaches, nears, blends, and becomes unified with God, who alone is perfect and without change in Himself.

Self Control

MAN CONSCIOUSLY desires something very much, and when it is obtained he discovers that this in no wise satisfied or lessened his desire, which is then transferred to some other object.

His conscious "I" is like a plaything, like a feather which is whirled around by different currents of air. Sometimes he is the sacrifice and sometimes the sacrificer, and he cannot hinder either.

His consciousness is but a single stage and but one form of expression of mind; therefore its dictum is but one and often untrustworthy. The influence and controlling power of his unconscious, the hidden and buried self, is immense over his thoughts and acts in the ratio of ninety-eight percent unconscious and about two percent hardly conscious. Restrictions, inhibitions, and obstructions which interfere with his full development of personality belong to this submerged part of his being.

A knowledge of the evolutionary progressive tendencies—the forward-moving and formative spirit of God within a man—would be the very basis of his improvement, evidently a directing force, other than his conscious or unconscious self at work through him and the universe. In all improvements of plants and animals, this working with the innate principle of their beings has been recognized and constructively utilized, but in man it has rarely been attempted.

But no real results can be attained if a person has not already developed a certain quality of character and intelligence which would make it possible for him to submit himself to facing his naked soul and the pain and suffering this often entails. To *buddhi*-man, or a man of developed intelligence who is nearing mental maturity, self-analysis and self-surgery would be of practical use; but neither of them are of any value to the undeveloped, dense, and obtuse. Without self-examination (*apa-china*), the weeds of whim are never cleared from his inner life. Only the understandable has significance; he cannot function where he does not understand.

What is the present duty or task he is avoiding, or what obstacles in his life's path is he unable to overcome? How many fulfilled adaptations to reality have resulted in his frustration and neurosis? And how he is seeking for satisfaction in the shadowy world of fantasy!

How situations and experiences, which should have been completed and finished long ago, are still dwelt upon and lived with! Images and matters which were once important but which normally have no significance for his later age are still actively influencing his present life. How frivolous attitude is maintained, where real seriousness is demanded! An inadequate psychic adaptation toward reality, which is quite to be expected from a child, is very discordant in an adult!

Thinking which adjusts itself to actual conditions is right thinking—a thinking directed by understanding. Such thinking is hard thinking, tiresome and fatiguing. A lessening of interest, a slight fatigue, is sufficient to put an end to the directed thinking, the exact psychological adaptation to the real world, and to replace it with fantasies is quite easy. Thus his inner life is dammed up to an unusual degree by the lack of application to reality. So, when he lets his unconscious "self" speak, he always tells us the most important things of his intimate inner life. In proportion as reality loses its hold, the inner world gains in reality and determined power, and now he turns toward his environment with diseased views.

Erotic impressions work in the inner unconscious life instead of the harmonious adjustment with the outer world, and in its stead his unconscious pushes forth symbols into his consciousness, tainting his dream life with the rising wish; and thus he plays hide-and-seek with his own self, asleep as well as awake. Injury to self-respect damages the ego-complex, and the breaking of self-respect cripples it. How to dig up and destroy this erotic root? Weak man stiffened with anxiety seeks salvation. How could we help him overcome the wounds and conflicts taking place in his soul, hurts which retarded his development and progress as a personality?

Self-control has limits which are all too narrowly drawn; calm is maintained at the critical moment, but certain results occur. The suppressed effect comes to the surface immediately afterward, seldom directly. A person who in official relations is polite, submissive, patient, and so on, soon turns his whole anger loose upon his wife or his subordinates. The suppressed effect creates compensations elsewhere. One may deem oneself freed of the conscious conflict; nevertheless, it lies invisible at one's feet and is stumbled over at every step. The technique of the apparent suppressing and forgetting is inadequate, because it is not possible of achievement in the last analysis—it is, in reality, a mere makeshift. The religious projection offers a much more effectual help; in this one keeps the conflict in sight—care, pain, anxiety, sorrow, or whatever its name be—and gives it over to the eternal supra-personal being standing in and above one's self—the Divinity.

Conscious recognition of the conflict is essential for its

overcoming. This conscious projection offers a double benefit. First, one is kept conscious of the conflict of two opposing tendencies mutually resistant, and through this one prevents a known trouble from becoming by means of repressing and forgetting an unknown and, therefore, so much more tormenting sorrow. Second, one lightens one's burden by surrendering it to God, to whom all solutions are known. One may properly ask oneself, "For what, then, is the deity useful if this efficacy consists only in the real transference?" Whoever to his conscious sin just as consciously places religion in opposition and accepts God's conquering grace, does something the greatness of which cannot be denied. Conscious transformation of an erotic conflict into spiritual values is something wholly worthwhile. Thought is no longer fettered by the emotional effects of the conflict, but able to rise to reflective observation and renunciation.

To bear a god within one's self signifies a great deal. It is a guarantee of happiness, of power, indeed even of omnipotence, as far as these attributes belong to the deity. To bear a god within one's self signifies just as much as to be God oneself. It is a strengthening of the individual against his all-too-great weakness and insecurity in real life. It is a song of triumph of the ascending soul.

Feelings of extreme insecurity overwhelm the individual who gives himself unconditionally to fate, which hides unknown dangers, and the perpetual hesitation of the neurotic to venture upon life is easily explained by his desire to be allowed to stand still, so as not to take part in the dangerous battle of life. Whoever renounces the change to experience to go forward with the driving strength of his own soul, by overcoming and thus enriching himself, must stifle in himself the wish for it and, therefore, commits a sort of self-murder.

This world is empty to him alone who does not understand how to direct his soul-force toward objects and render them alive and beautiful for himself, for beauty is first possessed within and then expressed without. It must first be seen within before it can be recognized without. The world offers boundless opportunities for everyone; it is rather the incapacity of the individual to accept its challenge, to bear its blow with understanding and love, to cause quickening of powers from within, which robs him of possibilities for growth into his Godlike stature.

The enormous indolence of mankind, which will relinquish no object of the past but will hold it fast forever, will have to be met and overcome. Whose power is it that binds the soul to earth and earthiness so firmly; and what cords are almost untearable; and how and who can set it free; and how could heart's knot be loosened and cut? And wherefrom does the heart, the unconscious, have an unquenchable longing for all the deepest source of our being, the sweetest feelings of home and happiness and the endless hope of all that is to be? And why, in spite of all our efforts, does our entire mental disposition and nature remain the same?

Life calls man forth to independence, and he who gives no heed to this hard call, because of childish indolence and fear, is threatened by a neurosis. Once the neurosis has broken out, it becomes more and more a valid reason to escape the battle with life and to remain for all time in the morally poisoned infantile atmosphere.

The entire being of man is demanded for the battle of life, and there can be no remaining behind; the call of the soul's destiny must be answered. The danger lies in isolation in oneself; solitude surrounds and embraces him, evermore threatening, evermore constricting, and evermore heart-strangling. He has wrenched himself from the world and is an actual escapist from reality and estranged from the rational actual existence.

Every weakening of the adult man strengthens the wishes of the unconscious, the dreams of his heart. What robs nature of its glamour and life of its joy is the poison of the retrospective longing which harks back in order to sink into its own depths.

Only in *sadh-sangat*—the company of lofty spirits—can his slumbering soul be roused and awakened. Then the willed introversion of his creative mind, though retreating before its own problem and inwardly collecting its forces, dives for a moment into the source of life, in order there to draw a little more soul-strength from the Holy Nām—the Living Word—for the completion of its task.

Painstaking work for a long time and for a remote object—God-realization—is not in the nature of a child-mind or primitive man; so, repeatedly, the power of fate will make itself felt unpleasantly when everything will go against his will and he will find himself not in harmony with himself.

Asceticism is forced sublimation and is always to be found where the animal or tamasic impulses are still so strong that they must be violently exterminated. The masked self-murder of the ascetic needs no further biological proof. Opposition of the soul within itself—a striving forward and striving backward at one and the same time—makes life simply most painful.

Our reason has been developed to enable us to maintain ourselves in the world we live in, not to help us penetrate the secrets of our own minds. The mind seeks for harmony within itself and between itself and the external word; it is in search of the truth about itself, by which alone it can live and prosper. But wisdom and gnosis dwell in the depths of man's own divine nature, sun-like and self-renewing, hidden in the mother's womb like the sun in the night. The Creative Word—the Holy Nām—imparts, like the sun through its rays, infinite life to all living creatures; it is the greatest fructifier and creator. One must learn to plunge into the river of life to become rejuvenated in meditation and thus return daily with added strength and soul-splendor to face life's tasks victoriously.

Spiritual progress thus attained involves a continuous adaptation to reality; and through conquest of reality, an increase of inner capacity and awareness and the creation of an ever-widening environment.

There is an exact relation of mind energy to physical and brain energy. Likewise, there is an intimate relation between mind which is conscious and mind which is unconscious, and this relation is reciprocal. The need and effort constantly to maintain equilibrium are fundamental properties of the human mind, without which it could not continue to exist and function normally. Equilibrium is what is called sanity.

Human actions are certainly determined, in the first place, by a mechanism built up in the mind and brought from previous states of life, carrying within itself the constitutional nature, the *subhava* of the individual and, secondarily, by the inherited mechanism.

No mind can occupy itself in the same channels for a long time without developing a complex, however weakly organized, and a characteristic affect attached to the complex. Complexes may be roused and temporarily dominate the mind. By acting upon these pre-existing elements in the mind, the external world brings about changes in consciousness. Thus conscious phenomena are constantly appearing as fragments of some larger whole; they cannot be understood without reference to that whole. Consciousness is essentially a superficial phenomenon mostly dominated by forces that are unconscious and subconscious. How can man emancipate his judgment to act independently of the bonds of complexes ingrained in his being?

The unconscious, the heart, cannot be awakened into consciousness unless the mind's barriers of prejudices and prepossessions are first broken down, and then the hitherto inaccessible subliminal mental elements become the part of consciousness in a unified synthesis. Unless man understands the history of his mind, he is not in a position to begin to estimate its existing significance. This includes, first, the history of the individual in the case of the mind—before birth, from birth up to adult life, and on to old age; and, second, the history of the race or, in the case of the mind, the development of the mind of civilized man from that of the primitive man, and of this from the animal, etc. And this thesis is still unwelcome to many who consciously or unconsciously regard it as a degrading admission of the continuity of the human mind with the minds of the beasts and savages. It is a distinct blow for them to discover that beneath all their pretensions lie the very ordinary elements shared in common by all. Every soul possesses in full degrees the historical evolutionary data in its inner strata, just as a tree does all that in the rings formed every year of its growth.

How can man escape his past, free himself from the "pull-backs," dissociate himself from his senses, extirpate all the prejudices, biases, bigotries, fancies, and phantoms, lay aside the guidance of his newly acquired intellect, leave behind all that belongs to the sensual and intellectual spheres, and extricate himself alike from what is subconscious, unconscious, and even conscious, which binds him to earth, and rise upward toward union with Him who is above knowing, an omniscient being?

Smoothness of human mind is constantly hampered by faltering purpose, mental conflict, and the refusal of the world to lend itself to the gratification of his heart's desires. What is ordinarily meant by "willing," involving conscious effort, is not only of no use in establishing the desired result, but actually has the reverse effect, which makes his last condition worse than the first.

Mind persists in taking short-cuts to unification. Incomplete knowledge may be regarded as complete, and false theories may satisfy the mind and drug it to sleep, especially if they minister directly to the gratification of the instincts—just as false views of the moral order and of God may satisfy for a while.

To grow, one must struggle; to win, one must be nourished from the source of life. Man's necessary regards and relations to both the world and the source of their origin are faithfully taken advantage of when he lives the life of truth and is exhausted by opposition from without and turns within to replenish his soul from the fountain and river of life—bathes his being in the *Ganga* of the Holy Nām, the sap-giving juice of life. To merge silently, freed into the stream of infinitude, is the greatest good of life, for Nām is the fathomless womb of all things; it is the form of the formless God, the shape of the shapeless; it is the heaven, the way, the path to be trod, the perfection to be emulated, the divine order with which one must come into accord. This is to be in *sahaja* state, when one is poised, relaxed, released; then one's action is spontaneous, free, and intuitive. Knowledge can be useful; reason will solve many minor problems; but neither can bring man into this kingdom of the spirit, the fatherland of the soul.

One must discover the joy of flowing along with the life-rhythm of the spirit, with divine nature's harmonious current. Then one becomes aware of the eternal in the transient. The transient reveals unending movement, ceaselessly unfolding order. Find the gateway to *sahaja* state in ourself, savor its ebb and flow, merge in its infinitude, spend yourself fully and be renewed again in the source of life each day—nay, several times a day—in meditation, until you are pure in heart. Then you will see Him in you—the Father of All Life, the *akal purkh*, the eternal person.

One must learn to pass beyond the three states of consciousness—waking, dreaming, and sound sleep, or conscious, subconscious, and unconscious states—into the reality behind them, from which they issue forth: the fourth state.

If one enters this superconscious *sahaja* state, his entire personality is transformed; the "crow" of mortality becomes the "swan" of immortality. His emotions are wholly integrated and satisfied; he is master of himself and divinely dynamic; health and harmony of the whole being are enormously improved; intellect is fully illumined, and he is the veritable embodiment of ethics and morality.

Sahaja state is not unconscious; it is full of awareness of one's self and God, both being one and inseparable. The whole mind is illumined—conscious, subconscious, and the unconscious. A man cannot enter this state unless and until the personal contents of the subconscious are first controlled, conquered, and then wholly extirpated by the fire of the Holy Nām. Hay and stubble—or whatever was only of a temporary nature—is all burnt up by Nām and disappears forever.

Mind must be trained to go beyond the time-space relationship and the conditions of name and form by the inward-pulling power of His Nām and grace; then the sense of sadness and frustration will begin to loosen its hold over the mind and man will have great inward peace, satisfaction, and spiritual strength, and become fitter to walk on the inner path. Meditation has a tremendous influence in building up the total personality of man and brings out the dynamic powers of the mind with all its latent possibilities. Only a man of meditation with the realization of God can successfully cope with all conditions and rise victorious and serve humanity best, both by example and by precept. The largest part of such a being belongs to the region of light, in which he is now firmly stabilized, and he takes counsel with no other but the Father of All Life within himself. Through the Living Light, when he sees Him in himself, all weariness and needs leave him. Unafraid in danger, untouched by desires, happy in misfortune, peaceful in the midst of a storm, he is elevated above ordinary mortals, on the same plane as the gods the *jivan muktas*, the living liberated. Adversity serves him, as well as fortune, and pain is like pleasure; the within and the without are one in him, and he one with the One.

The ignorant see Him in their imaginations outside the pale of nature. The learned see Him with the eyes of their minds as interpenetrating all the cosmos. But the illumined sage knows Him as his own self, of the self, and himself made in His image, and both being identically one and the same. But he sees and knows Him as though being seated in his own heart, the ideal companion of his life—the God in whom all men are one and in whom all men differ and are forever held apart. This "formful" universe was evolved out of God. If every being in it has its form and figure, can it be possible that the source, the author of myriad worlds and myriad forms in each world, is Himself formless? Can forms, whether sentient or insentient, come out of a being who is formless himself? He in whom all forms are involved, what is the form of His being, from whom they are all evolved? It is unscientific and irrational to imagine something coming out of nothing. The *karta-purkh*, the producing cause of the universe, is not formless. He is not only what marks Him out from man, but is also what makes Him common with man. He is man and plus, one is His immanence and the other transcendence, and this plus is the main, main fact. What marks Him out from man is first useless to man, and he sticks in meditation to that which is common to both—the human part. As the devotee develops himself by ascending in the inner path toward God, he appropriates to himself, little by little, the plus part which in the beginning was beyond his ken and capacity; it now comes within his reach, and thus gradually he becomes more divine in his nature and progresses toward the realization of the unity of human and divine in the Holy Nām, which is the form of the formless and support of all forms, and thus he knows he and the Father of All Life are one. He is at once most human and most divine, the ideal companion of man's inner life.

It is to this inwardly realized ideal companion—the *dayal-purkh,* ever-gracious and ever-compassionate being and ever-loving presence—that all his prayers, meditations, supplications, and worship are directed and addressed. It is He who forgives sins, whose substance washes the soul clean and makes it transparent and immaculate; it is He whose will is the moral law, and this God of inner experience and the cosmic God—the transcendental—are both one being, essentially and identically one. He is not a king to be obeyed or a tyrant to be appeased, nor a majesty to be adored, but a companion to be loved and a fellowship to be enjoyed. He is the fellow-laborer whose purpose must be fulfilled in and through us. They—man and God—are necessary to each other, and their relations are reciprocal and most cordial; they are "bosom-buddies," father and son dwelling together in the same abode.

The tiny human soul is flooded, vitalized, and fortified by the ever-enriching spiritual energies of its almighty companion in deep meditation, and it knows that someone cares, takes sides, is with him in his stress and strain, anguish and agony, suffers with him in his sin and selfishness, and is the friend, the lover of souls and all-forgiving Father—the divine person who lives and craves for his love. He who would hunger for such a God must learn to go within and condescend to sit at the feet of the holy *sat-guru*, who knows the hidden way in man's own constitution, who can put him on the inner path, and he himself will know Him within himself as the *sat-guru* knows Him.

Every seed cast into the earth for incubation undergoes a change—the baptism by water or moisture, later followed by the fiery baptism of the sun's rays. Water is emblematic of the body and its emotional life, hence the "world," the not-self in man, is alternately "destroyed" by water and fire and made newer. The *shabad*—the divine Word—transforms the man, the Word made flesh to Word made truth, thus changing his dark robes for the garments of white linen. The soul is deeply mired in the mud of materiality; she must be anchored to the Word within amid the constant flux of life, where there is no staying ground. The light of the Word consumes in both directions; it lights and it also burns and cleanses and makes the soul glow in beauteous glory. Freeing it from the dross it also painfully consumes the seed-thoughts of the lower self that bind the man to earth. The Word "intoxicates" the man with the divine wine (*Nām khumari*). Into the "grape juice" of his being, the water of earthly life, is now injected the fiery rays of the sun of wisdom from within, and the metamorphosis has taken place. He is now "born of the Word." His incarnation and reincarnation are his births into the bodies, his resurrection is his second birth, this time out of the body consciously into the spirit of God within him, and lo, he is a mortal no more. Though he lives in a mortal body, he is liberated and has his birth out of matter into spirit immortal within. *Amrit*, juice of immortality, the honeyed nectar of life, is his food, his sustenance to sustain, strengthen, and sweeten his entire being. Sweetness of life divine is his now.

He is risen out of the grave of the living body in his final resurrection—he is alive in death. This is dying before death. Death is dead, and for him there is no more dying. The wheel of birth and death, the cyclic law, the cycles of necessity no longer affect him. He is their master and ruler now.

Punch-shabad—five holy names—his soul must pronounce, ere the final release from the dungeon doors of mortality is realized. To pronounce holy names is to learn how to become equal in nature to Him to whom they all belong and thus ascend ever upward until the Word—consciousness of the Holy Nām—is fully entered into, where the twain are one and one twain. To become one with what one worships is the object of worship and thus to enter into its spirit and form both. For humanity to worship anything below the stage of its evolution is a step backward. In evaluation and appreciation of anyone, it is his qualities, merits, and worths that we give our heart's esteem to. A *guru* may physically appear as others do, but his way of approach to inner ideals is different from that of others. Not to bend our head in appreciation of his character is not to become like him. Saints and *sat-gurus* are the form of the Lord. Their very sight makes life's harvest most fruitful, their very contact is soul-stimulating, and their worship confers immortality and one is released from comings and goings and crosses safely the ocean of mind.

Nām is that omnipresent beingness (*hond*) which, being everywhere, is the cause of all life and living in all beings. Nām is God's all-pervading form in all forms, is the soul and support (*akar*) of the form. *Guru* does not give Nām, but shows the way to it and connects one with it. Humanity adores Him through myriad names, but the all-pervading and all-supporting and sustaining Nām is to be known and realized through the grace of *sat-guru*, the savior.

God before creation assumes this all-pervading form

through His Holy Nām, or Word. It is all-nourishing, all-pervading, all-supporting. To know and realize this form of the Formless One is the supreme end of life. By knowing this form of Nām, one becomes one with His form and immortal.

Without entering into the consciousness of Nām, sufferings and sorrow will cease not to smite the soul. Without devotion to Nām, fear will not leave. *Simran* of Nām (meditation on the Holy Name) is the greatest worship of God. By it the destructiveness of mind dies and its nature becomes pure (*nirmal*), without stain, and such worship is indeed most elevating.

Nām lives within all, but without *sat-guru* cannot be found. It is not local alone, but an omnipresent reality, pervading all locales and localities. Building of one's own personal worth and character is necessary. Without possessing a Godlike character, one can never blend with the being and form of God. While fires of greed and lust rage within, talk of meditation is sheer nonsense. He who has given up his egoism and self-seeking and has become dispassionate toward *maya*, in such a one's heart is His sight possible, and by His presence all fires of *maya* are extinguished and one abides in *sahaja* state. He is the holiest, the highest, the truest in whose heart the Lord of the Universe is seen and served.

Nām is the ship, its captain is the *sat-guru* who ferries the soul across through the power of the *shabad*.

Development of Consciousness

If, in reaching the mental life, we cast away or belittle the physical life which is our basis, or if we reject the mental and physical in our attraction to the spiritual, we do not fulfill God integrally nor satisfy the conditions of His self-manifestation. Not to abandon the lower to itself but to transfigure it in the light of the higher to which we have attained is true divinity of nature. Man's importance in the world is that he gives to it that development of consciousness in which its transfiguration by a perfect self-discovery becomes possible.

When we attain to knowledge or right consciousness, nothing essential in the eternal relation is changed, but only the inview and the outview from the individual center is profoundly modified and, consequently, also the spirit and effect of its activity. The universe and the individual are the two essential appearances unto which the unknowable God descends and through which He has to be approached.

The universe and the individual are necessary to each other in their ascent; always, indeed, they exist for each other and profit by each other. Universe is a diffusion of the Divine All in infinite space and time; the individual its concentration within limits of space and time.

The animal is satisfied with a modicum of necessity; the

gods are content with their splendors. But man cannot rest permanently until he reaches some highest good. He is the greatest of living beings because he is the most discontented, because he feels most the pressure of limitations. He alone is capable of being seized by the divine frenzy for a remote ideal. Death is ever with him; limitation invests his being and his experience; error, inconscience, weakness, inertia, grief, pain, and evil are constant oppressors of his effort.

To correct the errors of his sense-mind by the use of reason is one of the most valuable powers developed by man and the chief cause of his superiority among terrestrial beings. The complete use of pure reason brings him finally from physical to metaphysical knowledge. But the concepts of metaphysical knowledge do not in themselves fully satisfy the demand of his integral being. The question asked by one thinker of another is "What dost thou know?" not "What dost thou think?" nor "To what conclusion hath thy reasoning arrived?"

What is the significance of his little personal self in this vast universe? And what are the relations of God to him, and to the universe in which he lives? God dwells in all, indivisible, yet as if divided and distributed. He is indivisible and gives not an equal part of Himself but His whole self at one and the same time to the solar system and to the anthill. To Him there are no whole and parts, but each thing is all Himself and benefits by the whole of Himself.

We are infinitely important to God, but to us He is negligible. We alone are important to ourselves; this is the root of the ego, the original ignorance (*houmen*). Our own states of consciousness or mental standards are the only test of reality; all outside our orbit of view tend to become false or non-existent.

This mental self-sufficiency creates a system of false

accountantship, which prevents us from drawing the right and full value from life.

Our consciousness is only a small selection from our entire conscious being. It is a superficies; it is not even the whole of our mentality. Behind it, much vaster than it, there is a subliminal or subconscious mind which is the greater part of ourselves and contains heights and profundities which no man has yet measured or fathomed.

All illimitability, all infinity, all absoluteness is pure delight. All dissatisfaction means a limit, an obstacle. Satisfaction comes by realization of something withheld, by the surpassing of the limit, the overcoming of the obstacle—a self-possession whose other name is self-delight. And in proportion as the relative touches upon that self-possession, it moves toward satisfaction, touches delight.

In everything that is dwells the conscious force, and everything exists and is what it is by virtue of the conscious force. So also, in everything that is there is the delight of existence, and it exists and is what it is by virtue of that delight. Delight of being is universal, illimitable, and self-existent, not dependent on particular causes, the background of all backgrounds from which pleasure and pain and other neutral experiences emerge.

It is this vaster, profounder, truer-than-the-superficial consciousness which takes delight impartially in all experiences and secretly supports the superficial mental being and enables it to persevere through all labors, sufferings, and ordeals in the agitated movement of the becoming, because it sees harmony and beauty where we divided beings experience chaos and discord.

The nature of suffering is a failure of the conscious force of ego in us to meet the shocks of existence and a consequent shrinking and contraction, and its root is an inequality of that receptive and possessive force due to our self-limitation by egoism.

But neutrality to the imperfect touches of pleasure and the perverse touches of pain is the first direct and natural result of the soul's self-discipline, and the conversion to equal delight can usually come only afterwards.

In reality, there is a spontaneous working out of things from within, and the external shock and struggle are only the superficial aspect of this elaboration. The inner and inherent law of the one and whole (God, man, and the universe), which is necessarily a harmony, governs the outer and the processive laws of the parts or forms which appear to be in collision; to the supramental vision, this greater and profounder truth of harmony is always present. That which is an apparent discord to the mind, because it considers each thing separately in itself, is an element of the general ever-present and ever-developing harmony to the super-mind, because it views all things in a multiple unity.

To see things steadily and see them whole is not possible to the mind unless it is integrated; but it is the very nature of the transcendental super-mind—the Mind of God. Even to feel unity requires an abnormal effort, and to retain it, to act upon it continually, would be a new and foreign action not properly belonging to the mind. In the animal, and in man with his conscious mentality, this separative tendency of the mind induces it to regard itself as a separate existence and to take events and things separately. This is the error of the ego. "Things are not as they seem." Thoughts and things and forms are what they are by the force of the cosmic existence; they develop as they do as a result of their relation to it and to all its other manifestations.

Soul must be freed from the limitations of mentality and admitted to participate in the action of the divine super-mind. It is in the mind and its form of life and body that we exist on earth, and if we must abolish the consciousness of mind, life, and body in order to reach the one existence, consciousness, and bliss of God, then a divine life here is impossible. We must learn about the intermediate link between the two, which can explain them to each other and establish between them such a relation as will make it possible to realize the one-existence consciousness—delight of God in the mould of the mind, life, and body. The intermediate link exists; we call it *surt-shabad*, a principle superior to mentality, and it exists, acts, and procedes in the fundamental truth and unity of things, and not like the mind in their appearances and phenomenal divisions.

This principle superior to the mind and heart satisfies the condition in which mind fails. Whatever is in God's own being takes form as Nām, as self-knowledge, as truth-consciousness, as the Creative Word. And that self-knowledge and Creative Word fulfills or realizes itself inevitably in time and space.

Nām and form of God are inseparable. Totality of things is eternally subject to His gaze. We human beings are phenomenally a particular form of consciousness subject to time and space, and can only be in our surface consciousness, which is all we know of ourselves—one thing at a time, one formation, one poise of being, one aggregate of experience; and that one thing is for us the truth of ourselves, which we acknowledge. All the rest is either not true or no longer true, because it has disappeared into the past, out of our ken, or not yet true because it is waiting in the future and not yet in our ken.

Just as thoughts and images that occur in our mind are not separate existences to us, but forms taken by our own consciousness, so are all names and forms to this super-mind of God, which Nām, the Living Word, typifies and substantiates, combining within it the joy of the differentiation to the fullness of the joy of unity.

True fearlessness is ours when we enter into this background of fundamental blissful dualism in unity, where comings and goings, ups and downs, births and deaths, pleasures and pains, are seen as one and necessary for the growth of the soul. Nām has the power of lifting us out of the bogs of earth into the pure, high atmosphere of the divine state, out of the duality of mentality into the unity of the spirit.

The many are eternally dependent on the One. The eternal recurrence of the manifestation in time is a proof that the divine multiplicity is an eternal fact of the supreme, the *akalpurkh*, beyond time, no less than the divine unity; otherwise it could not have this characteristic of inevitable, eternal recurrence in time.

That which has come out of the divine must return to the divine. How we must change and what we must become in order to arrive at our true nature, through solidarity and self and God realization, is the goal of life.

We must be free from the discords of our divided consciousness, divided by ignorance and a separatist egoism. Abolition of separatist egoism and effective division in consciousness is the essential condition of the divine life; their presence in us is that which constitutes our mortality and our fall from the divine.

Perfection of humanity is elsewhere than in humanity itself. This earthly life need not be necessarily and forever a wheel of half-joyous, half-anguished effort. The attainment of God-state and the glory and joy of God can be made manifest on earth.

Mind cannot possess the infinite God; it can only suffer Him or be possessed by Him. The possession of God cannot come except by an ascent to the supramental planes, nor the knowledge of God except by enlightened submission of mind to the descending cleansing powers of the showers of the Holy Name. Mind clogged with the pollutions of mortality will be thus washed clean and drawn upward by the happy pull of the Word of God, and receive messages of the truth-consciousness of the Holy Nām, which will reveal its true divine nature and the law of its being (*subhava* and *sva-dharma*), ushering the *jiva* in *sahaja* state through gradual transformation of this nature. When the whole becomes known, the part no longer suffers from illusion of being an independent reality by itself. The grace of God has swept off barriers; both are now One Being.

Enslaved by our self-identification with the body, unable to exceed the limitation of our conscious ego, unable to escape from a particular movement of our consciousness in time, we remain bound; but when the action of the mind is consciously subordinated to the inner knowledge of the Living Word, the truth of the process by which egoism comes is known and not at all ignored.

Only the Holy Nām is firm and maintains a certain ordered constancy of figures and relations in the flux of things; it is the meeting place of the mind and super-mind of God, and it is the point at which they originally separated. When the veil is rent by the grace of *guru* and God, the divided mind, overpowered, silent, and passive to a supramental divine action of the Holy Word, gets back to the truth of things and loses its separateness. Then we find a luminous mentality, reflective, obedient, and inspirational to the ways of His Word.

Knowledge either of the whole or of the essence is necessary for the right knowledge of the part, or there is always an element of error in all human knowledge. Wherever part is, whole must be; wherever human mind is, mind of God must be. Egoism is the cause of our misery and poverty of spirit; freed from it we are sons of divinity.

It is impossible for a divided and individualized consciousness with a divided and individualized and therefore limited power and will to be the master of the all-force. The individual, by becoming one with the all-will and all-force which Nām is, can share the freedom of the all. Otherwise, the individual life in the individual form must be always subject to the three badges of its limitation—death, desire, and incapacity.

The energy of the life in the body has to support the attack of the energies external to it in the universe; it has to draw them in and feed upon them and is itself being constantly devoured by them. The life organized in the body is constantly exposed to the possibility of being broken up by the attack of the life external to it or its devouring capacity being insufficient or not properly served or there being no right balance between the capacity of devouring and the capacity or necessity of providing food for the life outside. It is unable to protect itself and is devoured, or is unable to renew itself and therefore wasted away or broken. It has to go through the process of death for a new construction or renewal.

The attempt at mastery creates always a corresponding reaction in the environment, which is full of forces that also desire fulfillment and are therefore intolerant of revolt and which attack the existence which seeks to master them. There, too, a balance is disturbed and a more intense struggle is generated, however strong the mastering life, unless either it is unlimited or else succeeds in establishing a new harmony through daily bath of renewal in meditation with its environment. It cannot always resist and triumph, but it must one day be overcome and disintegrated.

The fundamental necessity of the nature and object of embodied life itself is to seek infinite experience on a finite basis; and since the form, the basis, by its very organization limits the possibility of experience, this can only be done by dissolving it and seeking new form. Soul seeks its infinity by the principle of succession, by adding moment to moment and thus storing up a time-experience, which it calls its past. In that time it moves through successive fields, successive experiences or lives, successive accumulation of knowledge, capacity, and enjoyment, and all things it holds in subconscious or superconscious memory as its fund of past acquisition in time. To this process change of form is essential. Death is necessary because eternal change of form is the sole immortality to which the finite living substance can aspire, and eternal change of experience the sole infinity to which the finite mind involved in living body can attain. Unless the form-type is changed and the experiencing mind is thrown into new forms, in new circumstances of time, place, and environment, the necessary variation of experience, which the very nature of existence in time and space demands cannot be effectuated. This, then, is the necessity and justification of death, not as a denial of life, but as a process of life. Death, desire, and strife are the trinity of divided living. Only a completely unified life can enter the divine state here and now and loosen itself from mortality.

The struggle for life is not only a struggle to survive; it is also a struggle for possession and perfection, since only by taking hold of the environment, whether more or less, whether by self-adaptation to it or by adapting it to oneself, either by accepting and conciliating it or by conquering and changing it, can survival be secured. And equally is it true that only a greater and greater perfection can assure a continuous permanence, a lasting survival. It is this truth that Darwinism sought to express in the formula of the survival of the fittest.

The natural individual is a minor term of being, and exists

by the universal. Once this is discovered—as it is inevitably discovered by man, the mental being—his destiny is determined. For he has reached the point at which mind can begin to open to the truth that there is something beyond itself. From this moment his evolution, however obscure and slow, toward the superior something, toward spirit—God—toward super-mind, toward supermanhood, is inevitably predetermined. Such a one can meditate and draw strength from the source of life to become victorious.

As he moves inward through the meditative process, he becomes aware of an individual past, of individual lives that have created his *subhava*, his nature and character, and of which he is a development and modified reproduction, and of future individual lives which he is creating out of itself. He is conscious also of an aggregate life, past and future, through which his own continuity runs as one of its fibers. This, which is evident to physical science in the terms of heredity, becomes otherwise evident to the developing soul behind the mental being in the terms of persistent personality. This mental being expressive of this soul-consciousness is therefore the nodus of the persistent individual and the persistent aggregate life; in him, their union and harmony become possible.

In its upward ascent the soul grows toward the rule of conscious unity in differentiation, which is the divine law of the manifest Word of God—the Nām. We can only have some real power over so much of our existence as we are identified with by self-awareness through inner unfoldment; the rest must be governed by its own consciousness, which is subliminal to our surface mind, life, and body.

Profit cannot come by plunging down into our depths back toward the unconscious and the subconscious; it can only be by going inward where the Lord is seated and by ascending into that which is still superconscious to us and into the truth-consciousness of the Holy Nām that our unity can be fully established.

Knowledge can come only by conscious identity, for that is the only true knowledge—existence aware of itself. We know what we are so far as we are consciously aware of ourselves; the rest is hidden. So also we can come really to know that with which we become one in our consciousness.

The principle of unity is in the Nām alone; there alone is the conscious unity of all diversities; there alone the human and the divine are one and inseparable, and the human fully conscious of his divinity and immortality. Here, beholder is one with the beheld, and full unity realized.

Man, as he develops, becomes actively aware of the discord and ignorance that govern his relations with the world, actually intolerant of it, and more and more set upon finding a principle of harmony, peace, joy, and unity. The subconscious has this life of the All, and the superconscious has it, but under conditions which necessitate our motion upward. For not toward the Godhead concealed in the "unconscious ocean where darkness is wrapped within darkness," but toward the Godhead seated in the ocean of eternal light in the highest ethers of our being is the way to union.

Spiritual knowledge is a personal transcendent experience and cannot be imparted through the ordinary channels of mentality. It is an acquirement, an attainment through the grace of *guru* and God, and its effect completely transforms the entire nature and being of the seeker. In the waking state, the seat of the soul—the personal self in the body—is at the spiritual focus midway between the two eyes, just a little above the root of the nose and slightly inward. From this point its radiance spreads throughout the whole body and permeates every pore, giving life and vitality to every force and function. The soul does not move from this center; its rays directed downward enliven the entire frame and give life to every limb and ligament.

Just as the sun by merely shining, though millions of miles away from the earth, quickens the earth, gives it life, causes its seasons as the earth moves nearer the sun or farther away from it, so shines also the sun of the soul at this seat of the third eye. The two physical eyes show man the phenomena of the physical world; this third eye, when turned inward, opens to him the transcendent reality of the next world, which cannot be seen by the outer eyes. Through nine openings in the body, the soul contacts the outer world. They are: two eyes, two ears, two nostrils, one mouth, one organ of procreation, and one rectum, the ninth organ of elimination. Through these, soul's current is passing outward and makes it of world worldly. All this current of soul's energy can be collected and focused at one point, at the focus point of the third eye, and then turned inward and upward for greater unification and synthesis. The soul thus ceases to work on the physical plane; the switch is turned off the body and turned on within and, gradually passing through the third eye, moves into the astral and still subtler planes within.

The *sat-gurus* consciously draw their souls from the nine worldly windows and ascend into the tenth door—the door of liberation of the soul—from the caged condition of the body and enter into the land of spiritual transport, and quaff the nectar divine which "intoxicates" the soul, nourishes it, and makes it immune and proof against all conditions from without, and bestows upon it the lordship over all mental and earthly elements and elementals. What one has to do is learn how to turn the direction of the soul and the soul-current. The soul is now functioning and flowing outward on the physical plane through the nine doors, or five senses, and its back is toward the tenth door and the third eye. To turn the soul over and face the third eye is the task to be learned and realized. Take the soul from the earthly side and implant it on the other.

For spiritual knowledge one has to take away his attention from the world, collect and focus it at the third eye, and move it inward toward *gagan-mandal, trikuti,* and *daswan dwar* regions, step by step, and this is a task to be realized in time by the grace of *guru* and God. Turning the soul inward will make it see the self within and grow into consciousness of indivisible unity through direct cognition and experience. Closing the nine doors and collecting the scattered mind in the tenth will lead the true seeker into his true home in God. Here music of the spheres plays constantly and makes the soul realize this divine drama of joined lives of the individual with the universal; only with the help of *sat-guru* can this hearing of the Holy Nām be done and union accomplished. Finding entrance into the tenth door, the soul fully functions in its heavenly senses. It sees not with the physical eye, but with the inner eye, roaming around in rarer, subtler regions, but not with the physical feet. It talks to ethereal entities, but not with the physical tongue; it hears heavenly melodies of ravishing raptures, but not with the physical ears; it performs miracles of deeds, but not with the physical hands.

The spiritual senses of the soul accomplish these wonder-working feats. In the sphere of pure spirit, the soul talks and acts without the aid of physical organs and mental faculties. When this spiritual world becomes manifested and accessible to the soul, not for a single second does it care to tarry any longer in the lower worlds of mind and matter. So blissful are these transcendent realms that if once a being comes to know of them, he would instantly fly with all of his might to live in these incomparable abodes of bliss.

Sat-gurus alone know God and enter into the rarest essence of their being, but describe Him they cannot. There is nothing like Him to whom He could be compared and contrasted. They see Him; they know Him; they are one with Him; He is the very "warp and woof" of their beings. He exists, if anything exists at all; He exists if nothing else exists; His is the Primary Being—all others are derived from Him. He is above all scriptures, all the universes; He is seen in the heart of His devoted *bhagats* and devotees.

Spiritual knowledge is not imagination, for this, too, functions at the level of the intellect. It cannot give entirely new knowledge. In order to have more knowledge, one must have lesser knowledge. Man grows from lesser truth to larger truth; yet truth itself does not grow. Imagination can give us new combinations of various parts of our old experience; it can never give a thing which is entirely new in every part of it. A coinage of human brain, a production of his own imagination, cannot by its own nature bring about a vital change in his very being and essence that will be able to transform his animal and human nature and render them divine. The dawning of divine light of the Supreme Being in his consciousness helps him bridge the gulf that separates the finite from the infinite; its very touch and heavenly alchemy changes his baseness into the blessedness of His being. Whoever enters into the superconscious, transcendental fourth-dimensional state of *turya* himself becomes the glory of God and God of glory.

Philosophy deals with theories and speculation, and its organ is intellect. Ordinary "religion" deals with feelings, and its organ is emotion. But the science of spirituality (*Sant-Mat*) deals with reality, and its organ is *surt-shabad*, or transport. Spiritual knowledge does not consist of ideas and, therefore, does not develop from one man to another; it dawns in the bosom and being of the individual and is personal and not derived. It cannot be conveyed through thoughts; it is a personal, private transcendental realization of the self by the self, sight of the self by the self. This spiritual knowledge does not change. It is ever constant, the same at all times, for all mankind. It alone is true knowledge, because it is sure and certain. There is no possibility of doubt in it; it fills the whole being of the experiencer and is most effective in action; it guides and controls his entire life. Whatever he knows through spiritual union, he is sure to abide by. It has the power to make his life conform completely to its dictates. It cures him of all conflicts, all ailments, liberates him from all evil, gross as well as subtle. When the sun shines, darkness is gone; when true knowledge is realized, ignorance has vanished. When the bliss of the Being is imbibed, the pain of existence has parted and perfection of His glory has its sway.

The highest cannot be reached by mere talk or by reading scriptures or sighing over dead and defunct historical personages, but must be reached by the development of latent spiritual faculties of seeing, hearing, and speech. The "eye" of the soul alone can see His form and stand His grandeur; the "ears" of the soul alone can hear His voice and be raptured by the music of His life; and the "mouth" of the soul alone can utter the word that stills the storms of life and brings peace and joy to all.

That which possesses personality and is self-conscious (*chaitan*) is by common consent considered higher in the scale of being than that which is impersonal and unconscious. That which is unconscious of its own existence is very justly regarded as far beneath the self-conscious being in dignity, and we place the stamp of inferiority upon that which is unconscious (*jarh*) of its existence. Therefore the personal self of man, though imprisoned in nature, is still its lord and master, and even in doing evil its consent is necessary or nature cannot have its way. Can the conscious self of man have its ultimate origin in the unconscious? It may be the means of its growth, but it cannot be the cause and author of its being. The self-conscious can come out of Him alone who is self-conscious, the *akal-purkh,* the Eternal Being. The difference in the two self-conscious selves is not in kind, but in degree of manifestation. The finite self of man, though partially individualistic, still remains in vital though often unconscious union with God, whole and indivisible. The individual self is not of itself, for itself, and by itself, but of this Other, for this Other and by this Other, this full but hidden self in the heart of the personal being. He alone exists, self-centered in His own self-sufficiency, and all others are Himself in the worlds of form and reality. If all are He, it becomes our bounden duty to learn how to contemplate this Being with reverential love and devotion and realize our identity with Him.

Soul and God

WE HAVE TWO MINDS. One is the surface mind of our expressed evolutionary ego, the superficial mentality, created by us in our emergence out of matter; the other is subliminal mind, which is not hampered by our actual mental life and its strict limitations, something large, powerful, and luminous, the true mental being behind that superficial form of mental personality which we mistake for ourselves as the whole being.

Self-knowledge is impossible unless we go behind our surface existence, which is a mere result of selective outer experience, a fragmentary translation of a little out of the much that we are—unless we go behind this and send our plummet into the subconscious and open ourselves to the superconscious, so as to know their relation to our surface being. For between these three things our existence moves and finds in them its totality.

The real subconscious is a nether, diminished consciousness larger than our surface existence. But both belong to the inner realm of our being, of which our surface is unaware, so both subconscious and superconscious are jumbled together in our common conception and parlance.

Spiritual transformation from above is needed for us to possess our self in its universality and transcendence. In the

Nām—the Word of God—is the integrating light, the consummating force. The personal being lifted by its light and power can unite itself by the grace of *sat-guru* to the original Being it originally came from, overcoming the dualities of pain and pleasure, delivering from all fear and shrinking the mind, life, and body. And it can recast the contacts of existence in the world into terms of the divine joy.

Nām is the divine gnosis which creates, governs, and upholds the worlds; it is the secret wisdom which upholds both our knowledge and our ignorance; it is the poise of existence, the source of duality. It is that which being entered into, and when it is known, all becomes known.

Nām carries within itself a prospective as well as retrospective time sense, time vision, time perception. Something in it lives indivisibly in the three times and contains all their apparent divisions, holds the future ready for manifestation within it.

Here a clear vision of the ascending and descending stairs of manifested existence is commanded and the possession of the free power of ascent and descent becomes a spiritual prerogative.

The separatist ignorance of the ego strives to exist in its own right, although at every step it is evidently dependent on the cosmic power that created it. There is something in us, not in the ego but in the self and inmost being, that surpasses cosmic nature and belongs to the transcendent. We are self-existent and eternal only in God's eternity in the Nām—the Word—and by His self-existence in it alone.

An individual is something that separates itself from everything else and stands apart, though in reality there is no such thing anywhere in existence; it is a figment of our mental conceptions, useful and necessary to express a partial and practical truth. By the true individual we mean nothing of the kind, but a conscious power of being of the eternal, always existing by unity, always capable of mutuality. It is that being which by self-knowledge through Nām, the Redeeming Word, enjoys liberation and immortality.

All things, while different, are yet to come. There is an essentiality of things, a commonality of things. The commonality and individuality are true and eternal powers of the essentiality in the Nām that transcends them both; but the three together and not one by itself are the eternal terms of existence. The infinite and the finite coexist in and by each other in the Nām. There are three terms of the one existence—transcendent, universal, and individual—and each of these always contains, secretly or overtly, the two others. The transcendent possesses itself always and controls the other two as the basis of its own temporal possibilities.

Maya, moha, mumta—love for passing things and thirst for things—are put into the individual's nature by God, for nothing can endure if it has not a will in our nature, a sanction of Supreme Being, a sustained pleasure of the being, even though it be a secret or a perverse pleasure to keep it in continuance for educational purposes for our growth.

There is, too, somewhere deep down in us, the need of a total consciousness; there is in nature a secret universal seeking for the Whole Divine, an impulsion toward some entire awareness of delight and power of existence, a need of a Whole Being—a total knowledge. So long as the world is not divinely explained to us, the divine remains imperfectly known; for the world, too, is His, and so long as it is not present to our consciousness and possessed by our powers of consciousness in the sense of the Divine Being through the experience of His Holy Nām, we are not in possession of the Whole Divine.

Man's freedom is relative, and he cannot be held solely

responsible for the imperfection of his nature. Why is he attracted to the world and then repulsed by it? Divine omnipotence and omniscience has allowed this love of the world and self to rise in him by the fiat of His being; otherwise, they could not have been and would not persist in his nature.

A part broken off from the whole may be imperfect, ugly, incomprehensible; but when we see it in the whole, it recovers its place in the harmony. We discover a greater working behind our ignorant working and begin to glimpse its purpose in us; then only can we see and know what now we worship in faith, recognize wholly the pure and universal presence, meet the Lord of all beings and all nature.

To each a just limitation of an omniscient power, by the free will of that power, is granted in each evolutionary cycle of his appearance here, so that its surface energy shall be in exact correspondence with the work that it has to do, with its attempts, its allotted success, or its destined or necessary failure, proportionate with the balance of the sum of forces in which it is a part, and with the larger result of which its own results are an indivisible portion.

What is meant by our existence in *maya*, by our subjugation to her cycles, by our liberation from her? Salvation cannot be of importance if bondage is unreal, and bondage cannot be real unless *maya* and her world are real. If our being is that of God, our consciousness something of His consciousness, with whatever qualification, it is to that extent real. And if our being, why not the being of the universe?

Behind our self and spirit is the Self and Spirit of the All-Father, which takes account of every contact our self makes with the universe and draws a delight from this, first in the enduring, then in the conquest of suffering and, finally, in its transmutation that shall come hereafter. None else except this ever-loving and compassionate Being (*dayal-purkh*) could dare or bear to impose such experiences upon us and on itself—nothing else could turn them thus to His own utility and our spiritual profit.

There is a cosmic and individual utility in what presents itself to us as adverse and evil, for without experience of pain, we could not get all the infinite value of the divine delight of which pain is in travail.

It is possible, when we live inwardly in the depths, to arrive at a state of vast inner equality and peace which is untouched by the reactions of the outer nature and which is a great but incomplete liberation. For the outer nature, too, of mind, life, and body, has a right to deliverance. Even if our personal deliverance is complete, still there is the suffering of others, the world-travail, which the great of soul cannot regard with indifference.

There is no greater pleasure for man himself than a victory, which in its very principle is a conquest over difficulties. A victory in knowledge, in power, in creation over the impossibilities of creation, a delight in the conquest of an anguished toil and a hard ordeal of suffering is most welcome. And at the end of separation is the intense joy of union, the joy of meeting with the Father from whom we were divided and separated.

This joy of meeting illumines, integrates, harmonizes the significance of all knowledge. This supreme experiencer gathers together all experience in the truth of a supreme and all-reconciling oneness; a single decisive experience will undo a whole edifice of reasonings and conclusions erected by the logical intelligence.

Man is in his self a unique person, but he is also in his manifestation of self a multi-person. He will never succeed in being master of himself until the divine person imposes Himself on his multi-personality and governs it. Mind, in spite of its power, is often impotent before the unconscious and the subconscious, which obscure its clarity and carry it away on the tide of instinct or impulse. And often, in spite of its clarity, even it is fooled by vital and emotional suggestions into giving sanctions to ignorance and error, to wrong thought and to wrong action, or is obliged to look on while the nature follows what it knows to be wrong, dangerous, or evil. Mind, though it imposes considerable mentalized harmony, cannot integrate the whole being and nature.

Only the Holy Nām can bring about an inmost change and direct contact with our full being; nothing else can so deeply touch the foundation of our being and stir it, or cast the nature by its stir into a ferment of transmutation and mould the mind into a form of wholeness. The ego subjects itself to its purifying processes by being drawn and held to it, finally effaces itself, seems not to exist or exists only to serve a higher power or a higher truth or to offer its will and acts to the Divine Being as an instrument.

The true central being is the soul; it is by the coming forward of this true monarch and his taking up the rein of government that there can take place a real harmonization of our being and our life.

There is a long way from the surface to the depth in which soul, the psychic entity, is veiled from us, and this intervening space is filled with a subliminal nature and nature-movements, which are not by any means all of them favorable to the completion of the inward movement. The outer nature has to undergo a change of poise, a quieting, a purification and fine mutation of its substance and energy by which the many obstacles in it rarefy, drop away, or otherwise disappear. It then becomes possible to pass through to the depths of our being; and from the depths so reached, a new consciousness can be formed, both behind the exterior self and in it, joining the depths to the surface.

In entering within, one may find oneself amid a chaos of unfamiliar, supernormal experiences to which one has not the key, or a press of subliminal or cosmic forces, subconscious, mental, vital, subtle, or physical, which may unduly sway or chaotically drive the being, encircle it, in a cave of darkness or keep it wandering in a wilderness of glamour, allurement, deception, or push it into an obscure battlefield full of secret and treacherous and misleading or open and violent oppositions. Beings and voices and influences may appear to the inner-sense, and vision and hearing claiming to be the Divine Being or His messengers or powers and Godheads of the light or guides of the path to realization, while in truth they are of a very different character.

Thus one can be misled from the true way of the inner life and, seeking along false paths or wandering about in an interminable chaos of experiences, fail to find his way out into the true realization. Hence the necessity of a true *guru* who has realized the Truth and himself possesses and is able to communicate the Light, the experience, a guide who is strong to take by the hand over difficult passages, as well as to instruct and point the way. A strict obedience to the wise and spiritual leading of the *guru* is needed and is normal and necessary for all except a few who are specially gifted seekers as the result of such initiations in a previous existence.

Even so, the dangers will still be there and can only be surmounted if there is or there grows a complete sincerity, a will for purity, a readiness for obedience to the Truth, for surrender to the Highest, a readiness to lose or to subject to a divine yoke the limiting and self-affirming ego. These things are the signs that the true will for realization, for conversion of the consciousness, for transformation is there; then the necessary stage of evolution has been reached. A certain mastery can indeed be achieved, but mastery is not transformation, the change made by it cannot be sufficient to be integral.

As the crust (*bajjar-kapat*) of the outer nature cracks, as the walls of inner separation break down, the inner-light gets through, the inner fire burns in the heart, the substance of the nature and the stuff of consciousness refine to a greater subtlety and purity. The soul begins to unveil itself, the psychic personality reaches its full stature. The soul then manifests itself as the central being which upholds mind and life and body and supports all the other powers and functions of the spirit.

A governance, a guidance, begins from within, which exposes every movement to the light of Truth, repels what is false, obscure, opposed to the divine realization. Every region of the being, every nook and corner of it, every movement, formation, direction, inclination of thought, will, emotion, sensation, action, reaction, motive, disposition, propensity, desire, habit of the conscious or subconscious, physical, even the most concealed, camouflaged, mute, recondite, is lit up with the unerring Divine Light (*jot-narinjan*), their confusions dissipated, their tangles disentangled, their obscurities, deceptions, self-deceptions precisely indicated and removed. All is purified, set right, the whole nature harmonized, modulated to the holy key of His Nām, and put in spiritual order.

The light has to work in darkness or semidarkness on the hidden regions in us that are still in the night. The unconscious and the subconscious in us become susceptible to higher light, no longer obstructive to the fulfilling action of the conscious force of the Creative Word, but more and more a mould and a lower basis of the spirit.

Immortality is no longer a belief but an experience, a normal self-awareness, the close presence of the Divine Being,

His rule of the world and of ourself and natural members, His force working in us and everywhere—the peace of the infinite.

This transition is from nature as we know it to supernature in God. It is by that very fact impossible for any effort of the mere mind to achieve. Our unaided personal aspiration and endeavor cannot reach it; our effort belongs to the inferior power of nature, a power of ignorance, ego, and *maya*, and cannot achieve by its own strength or characteristics or available methods what is beyond its own domain of nature.

For a real transformation, there must be a direct and unveiled intervention from above, the downpour of the nectar of His Nām. Then a total submission and surrender of the lower consciousness, a cessation of its insistence, a will in it for its separate law of action, is completely annulled; and egoism (*houmen*) is no more.

When the ideal union is achieved, the two sets of principles become mutually attuned, vibrate synchronously, and are blended into one; when two organs of opposite polarity are united, a descent of power occurs. The measure and quality of that power depends upon the level of consciousness at which unity has been achieved; hence, the supramental conscious force of the Holy Nām called *nada*—the soundless sound—from above, and the evolving conscious force of the human ego called *binda* from below and behind the veil, acting upon the awakened awareness and will of the mental human being would accomplish by their united powers the momentous transition from the state of nature without to the state of the spirit within. There will be no further need of a slow evolution counting many millennia for each step, once the *guru* has shown the inner path to the gaze of the true Sikh—the seeker of life divine.

There are above us successive states, levels, or graded powers of being over-topping our normal mind, hidden in our own superconscious parts, higher ranges of mind, degrees of spiritual consciousness and experience. Without them there would be no links, no helpful intervening spaces to make the immense ascension possible. It is indeed from these higher sources that the secret spiritual power acts upon the being and by its pressure brings about the psychic transformation or the spiritual change.

They are domains of being, fields of existence, which are each a level of the universal conscious force of the Holy Nām. The *guru* will show the disciple the structural map of the ascent to the supramental summit, as a succession of separate steps each to be accomplished before the passage to the next commences. It would be as if the soul putting forth an organized natural individuality were a traveler, mounting to degrees of consciousness cut out in universal nature, each ascent carrying it totally as a definite integer, as a separate body of conscious being, from one state of its existence to the next in order.

When the higher descends into the lower consciousness, it alters the lower, but is also modified and diminished by it. When the lower ascends, it is sublimated but at the same time qualifies the sublimating substance and power. New capacities come as an inevitable result of the growth into a greater consciousness and a greater life, and that growth is part of the very aim of the spiritual being within us.

The will of the individual, even when completely free, could not act in an isolated independence, because the individual being and nature are included in the universal being and nature, and dependent on the all-overruling transcendence of His Holy Word.

Even when the outer and inner nature of the individual are unified in a harmonized spiritual consciousness, that still more external but occult part of him, in which his being is mixes with the being of the outside world and through which the outside world invades his consciousness, remains a field of imperfection. The spiritual inner consciousness has then to deal with these influences in such a way that as soon as they approach or enter, they become obliterated and, without result, are transformed by their very entry into its own mode and substance. The very tincture of the Holy Nām (*Nām de poh*) immunizes the within of a liberated soul, and the outside world has no power to effect, as the water does not wet the fowl, who lives in it but is insulated against it.

What we most suffer from in our outer life and its reactions upon our inner life is the imperfection of our relations with the world, our ignorance of others, our disharmony with the whole of things—our inability to equate our demand on the world with the world's demand on us. There is a conflict, a conflict from which there seems to be no ultimate issue, except an escape from both world and self—between our self-affirmation and a world on which we have to impose that affirmation, a world which seems to be too large for us, and to pass indifferently over our soul, mind, life, and body in the sweep of its course to its goal.

To harmonize ourselves with it, we either have to enforce ourselves upon it and make it subservient to us, or suppress ourselves and become subservient to it; or else we must compass a difficult balance between these two necessities of the relation, between the individual personal destiny and the cosmic whole and its hidden purpose.

But for the supramental being living in a cosmic consciousness, the difficulty would not exist. Since he has no ego, his cosmic individuality would know the cosmic forces and their movements and their significance as part of himself, and the Truth-consciousness of the Holy Nām in him would see the right relation at each step and find the dynamic right expression of that relation. In the pure state of spirit is the pure act of spirit and pure bliss of spirit.

A spiritual man is one who has discovered his soul; he has found his self and lives in that, is conscious of it, has the joy of it. He needs nothing external for his completeness of existence. When the spiritual delight of existence is in the whole depth of being, all the movements of nature will be pervaded by it and all the actions and reactions of the life and body.

A universal beauty and glory of being begins to manifest; all objects reveal hidden lines, vibrations, power, harmonic significance concealed from the normal mind and physical sense. In the universal phenomena is revealed the eternal joy of His existence.

Man's soul and God are in each other, live in one another, melt into each other, and yet, in a way, can appear as if different ends, sides, obverse and reverse of the same reality.

In our present life of nature, in our externalized surface existence, it is the world that seems to create us. But in the turn to the spiritual life, it is we who must create ourselves and our world. There must be the true self-realized within, if there is to be the true life realized in world and nature. To be fully is to be wholly conscious of one's being.

The universe finds itself through the individual, even as the individual finds himself in the universe; but he is capable of becoming more than the universe, since he can surpass it and enter into something in himself and in it and beyond it that is absolute—the God.

Man has created a system of civilization which has become too big for his limited mental capacity and understanding and his still more limited spiritual and moral capacity to utilize and manage a too-dangerous servant of his blundering ego and its appetites. To hope for a true change of human life without a change of human nature is an irrational and unspiritual proposition, an illusion and a mirage.

As winter's frosts make big cracks in the asphalt street, workmen force a tongue of flame upon the injured parts, and soon the warm glow unites parts that before were separated; so does the flame of the Holy Name—the *surt-shabad*—heal and make whole the injured and divided personality of man into a single unified individuality in God, when worked upon by the initiatory powers of the savior *sat-guru.*

Spiritual knowledge is not something that is gradually assimilated like intellectual understanding. It is a flash, the bursting forth of hidden transcendent light, which reveals all things in their true color and character in a moment of eternal consciousness; it transfigures and transforms our very being all in an instant. Men are turned into gods, made divine in no time. The evil leave their corruptions, the wicked become wise and saintly, the weak become strong and noble-minded, the sad and the sorrowful attain immediate gladness and serenity. Ganaka, the prostitute, becomes pure and pious, and so does Mary Magdalene. The murderous highwayman Valmiki becomes saintly, and the worshipful poet and author of *Ramayana,* Bidhi Chand, the hard-hearted robber, becomes humble and wholesome. Sadna the butcher instantly becomes Sadna the blessed and beautified.

The stuff sublime of spirituality alone can eradicate deep-seated evil tendencies of innumerable misspent incarnations and change completely the nature and being of man and bestow upon him resurrected and divine personality. As the summer shower falling softly upon the banks of violets cleanses the soot from the blossoms, so does the rain of His light falling upon the soul render it pure and virgin again.

In the deep forest glen a pure spring gushes gladly, and into this deep pool wild birds plunge and brighten their dull plumage. So does the soul dipped by Him in the pool of immortality (*amrit sar*) regain its original glorious grandeur of Godhead.

Every human heart has sought some feet to worship, some forehead over which to break its alabaster box, some presence before whom to pour out the entire fullness of the soul in devotion, its love, its hopes and tears. When offered to the savior's image in meditation, each sacrifice becomes a joy, each act of selfless service a sacrament, and all devotion a delight. With the eyes of mind the disciple sees the image of the savior; with the ears he listens to the holy names within, and with the speech of the mind inaudibly he repeats rhythmically the holy *shabads* given to him by the *sat-guru*, and by constant daily practice he moves to an ingathering of his whole being toward a final oneness, integration, and unity. The mind gradually delves down into its own depths and discovers its own source and unity with His mind, passing through the "narrow way" to become single at the *gagan-mandal*, and is inevitably flooded by the undiluted rays of this inner sun. Here the outside has become one with the inside in a single unity. The figure of the embodied *sat-guru* is fully lighted up and transfigured before him. He sees His face glowing brighter and yet brighter, and he himself grows less and less and seemingly fades away to find that He whom he worshipped is he himself now, inseparably one and the same. He has now seen the being in whose image he himself was formed and knew not, but considered himself as himself, by himself, and for himself. Now he knows they are both one, and he is the One; he has entered outside the condition of the flesh; though still inhabiting it, he is in the fourth dimension (*chautha-pad*), a state where he is neither conscious of the subjective nor conscious of the objective sides of life, but superconscious of the life as whole and undivided, therefore transcendent, indescribable, unthinkable—whole life of the whole man, in whose image humanity is formed.

From the inward fullness of life within, his whole being is coordinated—heart, mind, and body moving simultaneously and spontaneously, accomplishing wonders in the world. Sharing His full powers in a simultaneous process gives human nature its fullness of life and energy. Coalescing heart, mind, and body into an organic unity brings perfection of expression; otherwise one is strong where the others are weak. They are perfect only when they are united harmoniously in their spiritual relationships. Heart is not mind, and mind is not heart, and neither of them is the body. It is their direct opposition in their similarity that enables them now to come together in unity for His service. Each says something none of the others can say, and each is enriched by this unity in the midst of diversity. When mind mimics the heart and performs a part it is not fitted for, and the deliberative usurps the spontaneous, then man has artificiality and affectations. And when the heart apes the mind and the spontaneous usurps the deliberative, then he has chaos and anarchy. This disunion within the personality is always fatal to inner accord. Only in the basic root, the Holy Name, is their unity in diversity possible. The fundamental is that tone from which all others in the chord take their pitch, their quality. Therefore, gathering one's focus from the body to the *binda*, the seat of the third eye, and merging it into the *nada*, *gagan-mandal* brings the desired integration and wholeness. This first step on the inner path is essential for His vision—this uniting of the mind and heart in one great synthesis.

Guru's Grace

ALL HUMAN THOUGHT, all of mental man's experience, moves between constant affirmation and negation. There is for his mind no truth of idea, no result of experience that cannot be affirmed, none that cannot be negated. He's ignorant of his world in which he presently lives, which constantly acts on and through him, and on which and by which he has to act.

Our thinking mind is, in its very nature, an ignorant dealer in possibilities, not possessing the truth behind any of them, but sounding and testing each in turn or many together. If so, perchance it may get at some settled belief or knowledge about them, some certitude; yet, living in a world of relatives and possibilities, it can arrive at no final certainty, no absolute and abiding conviction. Even the actual, the realized, can present itself to our mentality as a "may be or may not be."

Our life-being is also afflicted by the same uncertitude. It can rest in no aim of living from which it can derive a sure or final satisfaction or to which it can assign an enduring value. Our nature starts from facts and actualities which it takes for real. It is pushed beyond them into pursuit of uncertain possibilities, and led even to question all that it took as real. For it proceeds from a fundamental ignorance and has no hold on assured truth; all the truths on which it relies for a time are found to be partial, incomplete, and questionable.

The history of human thought and endeavor is a constant breaking of bonds only to move always in the same spirals—enlarged, but following the same or constantly similar curves of direction. Human social and political endeavor turns always in a circle and leads nowhere; man's life and nature remain always the same, always imperfect, and neither laws nor institutions, nor education, nor philosophy, nor morality, nor religious teachings have succeeded in producing the perfect man, still less a perfect humanity. Straighten the tail of the dog as you will, it has been said, it always resumes its natural curve of crookedness. Christian love and Buddhist compassion have not made the world a whit happier; they only give infinitesimal bits of momentary relief here and there, throw drops on the fire of the world's sufferings.

Whatever changes are made in human life are of the form only, and these forms pursue each other in a futile circle, for the essence of life, its general character, remains the same forever. Our surface consciousness is constantly adding to its experience or rejecting from its experience and by every addition it is modified, and by every rejection also it is modified. All this experience is at bottom subjective, for even the objective and external is only known to mind in the form of subjective impressions.

In spite of our notice of no entry without permission to the external world, our inside is subtly and invisibly invaded by the world, enveloped by the not-self and moulded by it, its thoughts, its will. Its emotion and its life energy are penetrated by waves and currents of thought, will, passion, vital impacts, and forces of all kinds from others and from universal nature.

All manifestation depends upon being, but also upon consciousness and its power or degree; for as is the status of consciousness, so will be the status of being. Through consciousness, to know of the superconscious, the ever-compassionate complete God, Truth becomes the supreme need; and to discover the power and process of consciousness by which it can pass into super-conscience, the divine state, becomes the supreme discovery.

Human beings live as strangers to each other, at best tied by a very partial sympathy and mutual experience. We do not know enough, do not know others as well as we know ourselves, and that itself is little, even for those nearest to us. But in the subliminal inner consciousness it is possible to become directly aware of the thoughts and feelings around us, to feel their impact, to see their movements. To read a mind and a heart becomes less difficult.

There is a constant mental, vital, subtle, physical interchange going on between all who meet or live together, of which they are themselves unaware except insofar as its impacts and interpenetrations touch them as sensible results of speech and action and outer contact. For the most part, it is subtly and invisibly that this interchange takes place, for it acts indirectly, touching the subliminal parts and, through them, the outer nature.

We have to go into our inner being and learn to live in it and from it; the outer mind, life, and body must become for us only an antechamber. All that we are on the outside is really conditioned by what is within, hidden in our inner depths and recesses.

We find that the contradiction and struggles of our surface consciousness are largely due to the contrary or mutually discordant tendencies of our mental, vital, and physical parts, opposing and unreconciled with each other, and these are due to the discord of many different inner possibilities of our being.

Only in the inner subliminal being are the means to be

found of directly distinguishing between what rises from within and what comes to us from without, from others or from universal nature. There is greater power in our subliminal parts to overcome the time barrier, to have the sense or feel the vibration of coming events or distant happenings, even to look into the future. A certain sense of unity of the individual with the cosmic, a perception of the world held within one's consciousness, as well as of one's own intimate inclusion in the world consciousness, becomes frequent or constant as meditation progresses. A greater feeling of unity with other beings is its natural consequence. It is then that the existence of the cosmic being becomes a certitude and a reality and is no longer an ideative perception.

As meditation deepens, there is a spiritual emotion, a spiritual sense; there is an intermingling of oneness with Oneness, of being with Being, of consciousness with Consciousness, of delight of being with Delight of Being, of light of being with the Light of Being. There is a joy of intimate separateness in identity, of relations of love joined with Love in a supreme unity.

In our outer being we are the children of the unconscious; our inner being makes us inheritors of the higher heights of mind and life and spirit. The more we open inward, go inward, live inward, receive from within, the more we draw away from subjection to our unconscious origin and move toward all which is now superconscious to our ignorance—until we are stabilized in Supreme Being, the One ever conscious equally of the conscious and the unconscious things, who determines the operations of its indwelling energies and has power and dominion over both the conscious and the unconscious parts of all his creation and creatures.

Ego is the most formidable of the knots which keep us tied to *maya*; ego-sense clinches the division. Ego is the lynch pin invented to hold together the motion of our wheel of nature. The necessity of centralization around the ego continues until there is no longer need of any such device or contrivance because there has emerged the Full Self, the True Self, the Spiritual Being which is at once wheel and motion and which holds all together, the center and the circumference. The superficial or apparent man, the *jiva*, cannot go back at will to the real man within him, unless he has been connected by the grace of *guru* with the Word of God within as the fruit of a long and arduous self-training, self-deepening, self-heightening, and self-expansion.

As there are forces of truth, so there are forces that live by falsehood and support it and work for its victory. Only *satguru* can draw man to the divine light, truth and goodness. There are powers whose life is intimately bound up with the existence, the idea, and the impulse of good; so there are forces whose life is bound up with the existence and idea and impulse of evil, sons of darkness and division.

Subliminal experience shows that there are supra-physical beings embodying these forces that are attached in their root-nature to ignorance, to darkness of consciousness, to misuse of force, to perversity of delight, to all the causes and consequences of the things we call evil. These powers, beings, or forces are active to impose their adverse constructions upon terrestrial creatures. Eager to maintain their reign in the manifestation, they oppose the increase of light and truth and good, and still more, they are antagonistic to the progress of the soul toward a divine consciousness and divine existence. It is this feature that we see figured in the tradition of the conflict between the powers of light and darkness, good and evil, cosmic harmony and cosmic anarchy—a tradition universal in all ancient myth and religion and common to all systems of occult knowledge.

When we go back into ourselves very deep, away from surface appearances, we find that the mind, heart, and sensational being of man are moved by forces not under his own control, that he can become an instrument in the hands of energies of a cosmic character without knowing the origin of his actions. It is by stepping back from the physical surface into his inner being and subliminal consciousness that he becomes directly aware of them and is able to know directly and deal with their action upon him.

They may seize and drive a man at moments, or for periods; they may influence his impulses or his acts, or possess his whole nature. If that possession happens, he may himself be pushed to an excess of the normal humanity of good or evil, especially if the evil takes forms which shock the sense of human measure, exceed the bounds of human personality, approach the gigantic, the inordinate, the immeasurable. Their appearance does not extend higher than the lower supraphysical life-planes; they are "powers of the Prince of Air," air being in the ancient symbolism the principle of life, and therefore of the mind-worlds where the vital principle is predominant and essential. The vital mind, the mind of desire and sensation, is the creator of the sense of evil and of the fact of evil.

What is it in the human being that originates and gives its power and place to the sense of good and evil? All that is pleasant, helpful, beneficial to the life-ego is good; all that is unpleasant, malific, injurious, or destructive is evil. Its next valuation is utilitarian and social.

It is the soul in us which turns always toward truth, good, and beauty, because it is by these things that it itself grows in stature. The rest, their opposites, are a necessary part of experience, but have to be outgrown in the spiritual increase of the being. The growth of the soul is a growth out of darkness into light, out of falsehood into truth, out of suffering into its own supreme and universal *ananda*, or delight. As the inferior light is below good and evil (as in the animals), so the superior light is beyond good and evil. The surface mental individuality is egocentric; it looks at the world and things and happenings from its own standpoint and sees them not as they are but as they affect itself. In observing things it gives them the turn suitable to its own tendency and temperament, selects or rejects, arranges truth according to its own mental preference and convenience.

There are three types of mental individuality: that which is governed by the principle of obscurity and inertia, first born of the unconscience (*tamasic*); that which is governed by a force of passion and activity, kinetic (*rajasic*); and that which is cast in the mould of the *sattvic* principle of light, harmony, and balance.

The *tamasic* intelligence has its seat in the physical mind. It is inert to ideas, conservative and immobile. It thrusts away all that is new and likely to disturb it. The *rajasic* intelligence has its main seat in the vital mind and is of two kinds: one kind is defensive with violence and passion, assertive of its mental individuality and all that is in agreement with it, but aggressive against all that is contrary to its mental ego-structure or unacceptable to its personal intellectuality; the other kind is enthusiastic for new things, passionate, insistent, impetuous, often mobile beyond measure, inconstant and ever restless, governed in its idea not by truth and light but by the zest of intellectual battle, movement, and adventure.

The *sattvic* intelligence is eager for knowledge, as open as it can be to it, careful to consider and verify and balance, to adjust and adapt to its view whatever confirms itself as truth, receiving all that it can assimilate, skillful to build truth in a harmonious intellectual structure. Because its light is limited, as all mental light must be, it is unable to enlarge itself so as to receive equally all truth and all knowledge. It has a mental ego, even an enlightened one, and is determined by it in its observation, judgment, reasoning, mental choice, and preference. In most men there is a predominance of one of these qualities, but also a mixture. The same mind can be open and plastic and harmonic in one direction; kinetic and vital, hasty and prejudiced and ill-balanced in another; in yet another, obscure and unreceptive.

Relative good is the training imposed by world-nature upon us so that we may pass through it toward the true good, which is absolute. These problems are of the mind and the ignorant life. They do not accompany us beyond mind. As there is a cessation of the duality of truth and error in an infinite truth-consciousness of the Holy Name, so there is a liberation from the duality of good and evil in an infinite good; there is transcendence.

All other expedients will only be makeshifts or blind issues. A complete and radical transformation of our nature is the only true solution. A mental control can only be a control, not a cure; a total change of consciousness, a radical change of nature, is the one remedy and the sole issue. Since the root of the difficulty is a split, limited, and separative existence (*houmen*), this change must consist in an integration, a healing and wholing of the divided consciousness of our being, which He first gives us and then wholes us by the grace of His Holy Name.

Altruism is a potent instrument of self-enlargement and for the correction of the narrower ego, but it does not abolish it nor transform it into the true self, one with the all. The ego of the altruist is as powerful and absorbing as the ego of the selfish, and often more powerful and insistent because it is a self-righteous and magnified ego. It helps us still less if we do wrong to our soul, to our mind, life, or body with the idea of subordinating ourself to the self of others. To affirm our being rightly so that it may become one with the All-being is the true principle not to mutilate or immolate it.

To develop the *sattvic* part of our nature, a nature of light, understanding, balance, harmony, sympathy, good will, kindness, fellow-feeling, self-control, rightly ordered and harmonized action, is the best we can do in the limits of the mental formation. But it is a stage, and not the goal of our growth of being. To be ourselves liberated from ego and realize our true selves is the first necessity; all else can be achieved as a luminous result, as a necessary consequence. Spiritual call must be accepted as imperative and take precedence over all other claims—intellectual, ethical, and social—that belong to the domain of ignorance (the ego), for the mental law of good abides in that domain and can only modify and palliate; nothing can be sufficient substitute for the spiritual change that can realize the true and integral good, because through the spirit we come to the root of action and existence. There is the uplifting and change of the whole mode of nature itself, and not only some illumination and transmutation of the inner ways of the being.

Spiritual consciousness links the highest to the lowest through all the mediating terms, and achieves an indivisible whole—the presence of the timeless eternal (*akal-purkh*) in eternal time. The individual is a phenomenon, a temporal appearance in the cosmos. The cosmos itself is a phenomenon, a larger and more complex temporal appearance. The two terms "knowledge" and "ignorance" belong only to this appearance; in order to reach an absolute superconsciousness, both have to be transcended, not abandoned. Ego-consciousness and cosmic consciousness are extinguished in that supreme transcendence, and there remains only the eternal—the absolute.

Holy Nām links the three together. It is something by which nature is fulfilled in man and man in nature, and both find themselves in God because the divine is ultimately self-revealed in both man and nature, ego and the cosmos.

Through Holy Nām the *jiva*, the ego, is able to make its way upward from the lower to the higher gradation, taking up what it was into what it is and preparing to take up both into what it will be. Nām is the breaker of bonds, the seeker of new horizons, the disturber of the past and present in the interest of the future.

A complete evolution is pursued through a long succession of rebirths before one is fit for spiritual liberation. A perfect self-expression of the spirit is the object of our terrestrial existence. This cannot be achieved if we have not grown conscious of the supreme reality and the way that leads to the Holy Nām, for it is only by the touch of the Creative Word that we are transformed and arrive at our own God-self within.

The mental man cannot transform his nature, but he can control and harmonize it and lay on it the law of mental ideal, the moral law, impose a balance or a sublimating and refining influence and give a high consistency to the multi-personal confusion and conflict. He can be the observer and governor of his own mind and life, can consciously develop them; the rest will be done for him through daily contacts in meditation by the transforming and redeeming action of the Holy Nām, granting him peace which no earthly strife can shake.

Spiritual change begins by an influence of the inner being through the agency of the Nām inward to one's being. Nothing external can cause that transformation. Then our higher and inner being, now unknown to us, will become ourself; and the outer and the surface being, which we take for ourself, will be only an open front or an annex through which the true being meets the universe.

Our mental, physical, vital existence, when spiritualized, can and does become much richer, greater, more powerful, and more perfect. In their divine change they break into possibilities which in their unspiritualized condition could not be practicable or imaginable.

Physical science with all its achievements may accomplish comforts and plenty, but it can never achieve happiness and fullness of being for the human race. Our true happiness lies in the true growth of our whole being, a victory throughout the total range of our existence. Mind itself is not enough; even its largest play of intelligence creates only a qualified half-light.

The objective assumes value only as it has a relation to the soul. It is a field, an occasion, a means for the soul's progression in time. The objective is a ground of manifestation for the subjective. The subjective and objective are two necessary sides of the manifested reality, and of equal value.

Being is not separate from the becoming, but present in it, constitutive of it, inherent in its every infinitesimal atom and in its boundless expansion and extension. Becoming can only know itself wholly when it knows itself as being and not apart from it. Soul is an eternal portion of the Supreme, and not a fraction of nature. Neither the cosmos nor the individual consciousness is the fundamental truth of existence, for both depend upon and exist by the transcendental Divine Being.

There are two cooperating forces working within our being, an upward-tending force from below (*binda*) and an upward-drawing and downward-pressing force from above (*nada*). It is this upward-drawing action and this pressure, this insistence from above, which explains the constant influence of the spiritual, mental, and vital worlds upon the physical plane.

Vital worlds are the natural home of the powers that most

disturb human life. Without learning of the inner path from the *guru*—the king's highway to His heaven—every silence and meditation will be a descent into the subconscious and will not help us to explore this region, for it will plunge us into incoherence or into sleep or a dull trance or comatose torpor. Our conscious awareness is of utmost importance. For the subconscious is the unconscious in the process of becoming conscious. To penetrate into its dark depths, to bring in light and establish a control and conquest, is indispensable for the completion of any higher life, for any integral transformation of our nature. And then it is possible to realize our persistent existence in time, as well as our eternal existence beyond time.

As man learns to look within to discover his inner being, his spiritual self, to aspire, to overpass earth and her limitations, he must learn to contact the force that lifts him up. As he grows more and more inward, his boundaries mental, vital, and spiritual begin to broaden; the bonds that held life, mind, and soul to their first limitations loosen or snap, and man the mental being begins to have a glimpse of a larger kingdom of self and world, closed to the first-earth life.

An action from within and an action from above can overcome the predominance of the material formula, diminish and finally put an end to the power of the unconscience, reverse the order of the consciousness, substitute spirit for matter as his conscious foundation of being, and liberate its high powers to their complete and characteristic expression in the life of the soul embodied in nature.

There are many stages that are to be entered into on our inner journey. At every point of the ascent there can be a breaking out of the spirit at that particular level of its full manifestation and absorption of our being into that state, an intensity of the heart, a total silence of the mind. A single absorbing passion for His Holy Name and sight would be enough to bring about that culminating movement, until the two coalesce and blend.

There is a downward attachment so strong, unless pulled by the stronger upward power and overcome, as to compel the being to hasten at once to a resumption of the physical life, because his natural formation is not really fit for anything else or at home on any higher plane. On reaching a certain stage of evolution through ascent, man expresses himself in identical terms all the world over: the wise, the illumined of all times and climes, agree in fundamentals, though they have never seen one another nor even heard of one another.

Nothing can soil fire. The fire of His Holy Nām, the Word, purity incarnate, purifies everything. The search for the Nām must be made within the human body through mercy and grace of the *guru.* The human body is like the earth, where the worshipers dig deep for the divine jewel: the deeper one can dig, the more copious becomes the ore he obtains. A man ought to have only as much of material food as he can hold and digest, and the same rule applies equally to spiritual food. As the hunger for His bread grows, so grows the supply that satiates the soul.

As a spark would kindle a piece of charcoal, and as the charcoal glows its blackness goes, so does the blackness of the heart go when the spark of His Holy Nām sets it on fire and destroys forever all earthly affectations and renders it pure and immaculate. Thus does the inner being become calm, rid of all germs, all its cumbrances cut, free from pain and pining, and sees Him who lives within the bright space of the heart, and becomes one with Him.

As the child "quickens" in the womb or the sap "quickens" in the tree, the "quickening" is always the presage of a new birth. So is man's inside quickened by His substance and His presence, and this is the herald of a new and complete life. When the sweet babe is healthy within, a soft rosy bloom appears on the cheek without; when ripeness enters the heart of the grape, a purple flush appears on the surface of the cluster. So it is with man, when he is born of the Word of God by the grace of *sat-guru*—the embodied way-shower and helper. He who laid the foundations of the universes and prescribed their limits, He who made the vehicles of the souls and put the immaterial souls into the material bodies, has also the power to break those limits and withdraw the embodied souls into oneness with Himself again. And when this power is granted to His sons, they also have the power to lay down their vehicles and take them up again at will and be with the Father all the time at their sweet wills. He who has driven the life-force, the *kala*, from amoeba to man in this gross world has also the power and *shakti* to transform men into gods.

To set the soul free from the bonds of matter and mind for the realization of spiritual synthesis, the body and the mind have to be put into perfect rhythmic relations with the Word within and trained to a condition of perfect harmony with the rhythm of the universe, which harmony leaves the soul undisturbed and disentangled from bodily trammels and mental complexes and helps it ascend inward into the core of being and oneness with Him. Until this rhythm is realized, all irregularities make of the body and mind a discord, an encroaching element of disturbance that pulls the soul earthward.

The power to transport the soul Godward must exceed the power of *maya* to drag it earthward, and when this conscious connection is made and man is joined to the Word of God within, then tremendous waves of spirituality and light divine are set in motion, which spread in all directions and definitely influence the lives of men. Because they come from the heart of being, they are irresistible and of greatest value and worth in healing the hearts, minds, and bodies of being. In the presence of that which brings release from desire, we no longer strive and feel tense and tired. The personality is brought into a state of unity and self-completion and is liberated from desire, freed from tension, and stimulated to joyous spontaneous expression.

Listening in of the *anahat-shabad*, the soundless sound, with the ears of the mind, repeating with the mind the Holy Names—the *guru mantra* imparted by the savior *guru*—and seeing with the eye of the mind the form of the *guru*, in time affect a synthesis in which the whole being of man is unified, and all distinctions of outer and inner mind are completely gone. The mind as the minor side of man and heart as the major are in this state fully coordinated and made one. Then the light of God shines without interruption, laving and bathing the entire being of the worshiper.

Such meditations daily performed grant stable equilibrium to the consciousness, and it becomes fixed and full of joy to know the eternal, who bestows upon her His *prem-bhava*, the heartfelt devotion to Him, a strongest sense of inner attraction to Him. In the depths of the soul glows a light which is never seen without, and an original sound is heard coming from the very heart of the being, a sound that has no syllables, and a perfume breathes out which stays with the worshiper and sanctifies the surroundings he dwells in. He has not yet passed on from the state of three *guna-maya* or nature to the spirit of God within him. He is in the heart of that nature, in the state of *sattvic* luminosity, and being pure in heart, he is given a *darshan* or sight of Him who lives in all hearts.

In this state his vision is steadfast and his power of judgment unwavering; a certainty consciousness prevails. Here mind is one, undivided. In such a mind is unity; it is whole, and the whole mind sees the whole man. By identity of consciousness and spirit of man is the consciousness and spirit of God to be realized, and in no other way. Here *prem-ras*, the nectar of love divine of the soul for her Lord, is enhanced by the highest complimentary differences under circumstances of tenderest intimacy as the meditation matures.

Soul does not and cannot know all of God; for He is *agam*, the absolute and the eternal being. Her knowledge of Him is so far as He is related to the being of each individual. Human faith springs from this actual knowledge; this faith feeds knowledge, and knowledge feeds faith, like clouds feeding the oceans and oceans the clouds. Soul becomes conscious of immortal life with the Father; it needs no outer proofs of life eternal. Union of the soul with the body and its conscious separation from it is no longer a sealed mystery. Mystery is just a nickname for human ignorance. There is no mystery for him who is able to withdraw his senses from objects and is capable of placing them quiescent in the mind and withdrawing the mind from the images obtained by the aid of senses and placing it quiescent in the heart. Thus, the whole being unified, he sees what eyes cannot see, hears what ears cannot hear, and speaks what tongue cannot utter. Just as the mercurial covering at the back of the mirror enables the mirror to reflect forms, tincture of the Holy Nām (*Nām de poh*) working on the mind enables it to be merged with the mind divine and become one and reflect omniscience.

As the letters of the alphabet, which stand only in sounds, have been formed and are the cause to learn the intellectual powers, so is the *guru murat*, the form of the *guru*, substituted for the formless God, that we may know by experience the fathomless being of His existence whose form is revealed only in and through His Nām—the Word.

The mortal form of the *guru* whose liberated spirit awakens the spiritual form of our God in our soul, though occasionally confused before, is now on the whole clearly distinct and separable in thought. They are perceived by separate faculties. The mortal form, so far as it is a mortal object, is perceived by the senses, by the surface sight, speech, and hearing; but not so this inner form of the inner vision, where *guru* is Govinda (God), and God is *guru*, and both are seen as *One.*

The vision in the supernal consciousness with its accompanying blaze of splendor cannot take place except by, in, and through the worship of God as *guru*, the best representative of highest manhood of liberated and perfected humanity, and through his grace and inner help. The false notion of a separate and atomic self apart from God and having interests of its own distinct from Him dominates him no more, as it did for a long time, leading to the most terrible struggles and miseries—although all necessary and educational. This fight of the ego against other egos has ended for good, as has the other everlasting doubt as to where may be found in the midst of chaos an abiding reliance, the resting place for his ever-restless self.

Divine Truth

God is not universal reason or ineffable being or absolute good or morality or a tendency and trend that makes for righteousness, but the being who brings into being all the visible and invisible beings and things, and is in each as the Soul of its soul, the Being of its being, and above all is *akal-purkh*, who is the perfect artist, perfect lover, and perfect geometrizer and indweller in the human spirit. He is the common Father of all, fashioning worlds and supporting them from within, a personal Father to each, capable of being loved and honored and who in turn loves and values His children. He is without fear and without favor, has no enmity with any. He is above time, without birth and death. He is in Himself and by Himself and alone. He is known through the grace of the savior *guru*.

God is indivisibly one above every other being, however highly placed or conceived, such as Brahma, Vishnu, Shiva, Rama, Krishna, Buddha, Mohammad, or Jesus. He is the highest moral being, Who has inscribed all men with His Name or moral presence. He is not a God belonging to any particular people, but is the dispenser of life universal. No one created Him, and He has no image of Him; to worship Him in idols and images is derogatory.

He has no father, mother, son, or daughter. In all forms He

is manifest. He is the light in all hearts, and by His light He fills all the universes. He is beyond all the scriptures and the universes and is seen only in the heart of man, and His sight destroys all miseries, banishes all superstitions, brings peace and joy of life immortal to the worshiper. He is the storehouse of all qualities, mine of all merits, eternal giver of gifts and of ever new values to life.

The ways to realize Him in oneself are not many, but only one, and that way is not the way of knowledge or the intellectual concepts of various creeds. To be fully sure of His presence from within, entering into oneness with Him and experiencing this unity of the two is essential. The foundations of man's uplift are not laid on such shortcuts as miracles, mantrams, and mysteries, but on man's own humanity, his own character. It is the character alone which helps him in moral crisis.

Mysticism can be and often is a pure bluff for the obvious purpose of exploiting the credulous. It often promises the kernel and offers the rind. Man's ultimate aim is the development of the fullness of Godhead involved in his being. Full effort means full progress, and full progress brings full attainment.

Our savior *gurus* thought it necessary to take in hand a whole people for a continuous course of training in wisdom and experience spread over many generations before they could be sure that the people so trained had acquired a character of their own. This is the reason why in Sikh religion there have been ten founders and exemplars instead of only one. No innovator, no reformer, prophet, sage, or savior can arise out of the heart of a people or a nation unless it is prepared for that specific knowledge which he comes to impart. The Buddha will not be born in Berlin, nor a Shakespeare among the Hottentots; nor shall a Gandhi rise amongst the Yankees or an Edison appear in the midst of Australian bushmen.

Man does not start life with a blank character. He has already existed before he is born; he inherits his own past, as well as that of his family and race. All this goes to the making of his being and has a share in the moulding of his nature. But this is not all. He is given a will with which he can modify the inherited and acquired tendencies of his past and determine his coming conduct. If this were not so, he would not be responsible for his actions. This will again is not left helpless or isolated; through the grace of *guru* and God's Word within him, it can be attuned to the supreme will of the Father of all life. Then he acquires a force with which he can transcend all his past, transform it, and acquire a new character.

Regeneration comes when, at the call of grace, he begins to subject his tiny self to the Highest Self that is God, and his own will is gradually attuned to His supreme will until he feels and moves just as He wishes him to feel and move. One's own efforts and devices do help, but at their very best they are limited, and one can never fully transform his own nature by them alone. God's grace is all-sufficient and is essential and most needed. His Holy Nām is the *aqua nostra* which dissolves everything effete and renders the soul pure.

What we call ourselves, He is the life of it and the sole soul of it; hence He can never be seen apart from our own self, as we see others apart and separate from ourself. Heart's eye alone sees Him in the self and the self in Him through *guru's shabad* (the Word) alone in this inner sight, by which the unseen is seen as *sahaja* state and entered into and realized. The germ of His light, placed within our breasts, when fully developed is capable of union with its source in Him. The selfhood is from Him and is indestructible. The self has entered conditional existence for its growth, unfoldment, and union with Him. Just as we come to know ourselves in meditation apart and different from all that is perishable in us, so in us is He seen as the sole support and substance of ourself—the self of all selves.

The universe is born of His will, and good and evil are placed in the very nature and heart of it by Him, and they are the means for the growth and unfoldment of souls. All the three worlds are for our edification. All obstacles, problems, and difficulties are stepping stones for soul's own elevation and enrichment. Battling with them makes the soul stalwart, and winning victory over them gives the soul the crown of manhood.

This world is not an illusion; it is most real. It is He Himself in constant and ceaseless flow of His being in ever new becomings. All His universes are true and real. This world in which humanity lives has a rational structure and is knowable by man. Its right knowledge is very necessary for the growth of the human soul and its enrichment. All its activities are measurable and display an orderliness expressible in definite laws. These laws are fixed and changeless, and human thought can anchor there without fear of partiality or prejudice. All things are related to man, and he is related to all things.

Perfection can only be realized in human manifestation of the soul. Human existence is the most precious; in all others God is concealed, but only in man is He revealed, when *shabad* (the Word) awakens him. He of all beings is more "bored" with himself and thus capable of progress and progression. God is the spirit-ground of time, upon whom time depends and whose activity makes Him functionally related to the temporal order. God is real being, and stands in real relations to each being's temporal experience.

Every personal self is itself and not another's, and bears a unique individual relation to the Father of all selves. Every doer is limited by his own character. God does not transform, differentiate, or fractionate Himself and so cease to be God in the human self. He is ever indivisible (*akhand*), though unknown through his *maya* to the differentiated and fractionated self.

All enrichment of man has come through the discovery of truths already operative in nature and through the harnessing of these truths for human needs, service, and uplift. The evergrowing powers of an individual or a nation or humanity are the powers of truths made practical for mankind's welfare. All creation is progress in realized values, a continuity of life in greater manifestations; memory must continue if the same active self relates the old to the new, thus holding old values realized, retaining the expertness self has gained, and being enabled to seek new values beyond.

Dayal purkh, the compassionate, ever-gracious Father, has unfathomable interest in each creature, whom with infinite patience, skill, and loving care He has thus far sustained, invoked, persuaded, and even pushed on its arduous way toward rationality and morality. Moral values can subsist ultimately only in persons; they alone can be consciously conscious of them. No perfect God would produce free beings to cut them off at death.

Soul's elevation and enrichment also come through living in harmony with the laws of one's own being, operative in all departments of life. As all insentient things and beings are subject to the laws of God working in their respective natures, so is sentient man also subject to His will and laws. Man cannot violate the law and not suffer from the consequences. He has no power to create such laws in nature. They are there for him to discover, know, and work with. He has the choice to work with them, but he cannot indefinitely go against them. As he sows, so he reaps, and similar becomes his nature, temperament, and future.

As the sparks are one with the fire before differentiation takes place and gives them their separate existences, so are the souls with God before manifestations. As the souls have grown and unfolded, so have the minds and bodies and other vehicles become rarefied and complex. All experience is the becoming expert by experiment. Our mistakes are not God's, but He permits their possibilities in our natures and souls.

The personal self precedes the birth of all its vehicles and survives, richer or poorer, the demise and death of all its instruments, its component parts. Human *jiva,* the personal self, is not *anadi,* beginningless or endless, nor is it God; it is like God, self-conscious, but is begotten and limited in its scope. Speaking in terms of evolution, *jiva* is capable in time of developing fullest access into *atma,* the divine person, and becoming one with His form. God, who begets the *jiva,* abides within it. He is the very warp and woof of the personal consciousness; He delegates all His powers in embryo.

In the ocean of divine consciousness and being, through the creative power of God, the Holy Nām, a center, a nucleus of personal self is born which becomes walled by mind and matter and feels having a separate existence of its own beingness (*houmen*). This "I," "me," and "myself," this *meum* and *tuum,* is the foundation rock of personality. The *houmen,* or sense of separate existence or personality, is the cause of man's separation from the spirit of the Creator, the Father of all life.

Maya-mumta, the love of external and perishable things, is given to man by His divine decree for his experience, growth, and enrichment. Richness of his personality accrues from increasing commerce with ever-widening consciousness and environments. Finite creators are ever dependent in their activities upon a never-failing other, and this is the divine person who is the alpha and the omega, the beginning and the completion, of the finite. And the non-ego is the dynamic source of that stimulus, external to the knower, which by friction and opposition causes growth of the ego as it overcomes its environments. As long as he is bound by *houmen*, this sense of separateness, that long is he to have birth followed by death, pain by pleasure, and to remain fettered in the meshes of mind and matter and be dominated by mortality.

Jiva's personal activities and interests determine his nature and character through experience. His living affects his life, and his life his living, thus forming his basic nature, his *subhava*. And as many evils and demerits as he has in his character, that many are the chains that bind him to the wheel of existence. By the grace of *guru* he learns to die while still living—yes, die to his *houmen* sense of being a separate being by itself. This living death ushers him into a life which is whole, holy, and complete. He must learn to harness all powers of his body and mind and unify them in such a single-state of being as to cause illumination of his self, so that the candle of his life will be lit up and light will shine inside of him in the hollow of his heart. Dedication of his heart and mind to His purpose and rejoicing with equal-minded impersonality in the pairs of opposites as the wheel turns will enable him to transcend the realm of duality and be the recipient of His grace and thus enter into the synthesized state of his fullness of being—the *sahaja* state.

Jiva must learn to rejoice in His will and never abandon truth, even when in extreme pain and poverty, taking gold and clod of earth alike, never swerving from His path even for the sovereignty of the three worlds. As same-mindedness toward duality or the pairs of opposites is established and impersonality and equality realized, he shall easily enter into the state of unity where there is perennial peace, living light that nourishes his whole being, and joy of the eternal divine state. In the *sahaja* state there is no defeat, but victory and triumph;

no distress, but all delight; no evil, but all good; no sorrow, but all serenity and bliss and immeasurable gains in daily life and living. Once a devotee has entered this state and stabilized himself in it, all mortal weakness is a thing of the past; he shall neither faint nor falter anymore, but stand stable like a big rock in the swirling waters of the ocean of life. All illusions and superstitions have disappeared, all fetters are cut, chains bind him no more to earthy slavery. This *param pad*, the supreme station, alone is immovable and full of beauty and bliss.

Each *jiva* is capable of becoming one with the Father within, when all its dirt and dross is washed away. By good deeds alone, one cannot enter into the state of *sahaja*, and without entering *sahaja*, fear never leaves one. In fear, *jiva* is polluted and has to be washed and purified. Mind is stained, and *shabad*—the Word—alone can make it clean and immaculate and bring the unification and wholeness of mind needed for the *darshan*—the sight of God within the soul.

One must live the life of full giving and receiving—the natural life—and seek its sublimation and complete fulfillment through pursuit of the moral law. Be in the world, deny it not; neither run after it, nor away from it; use all its values and worths for soul's growth and God's glorification. Sanctify every relation. Neither the mind nor the *maya* is destroyed; through the lifting power of the Holy Nām one can transcend them both and cross the ocean of birth and death, and enter the immortal state.

Running in diverse directions for salvation is never fruitful. Without Nām, the wandering, restless mind never comes to peace. The liberator is within our own heart and being. Ambrosia, the nectar of the Nām, which strengthens the soul and purifies it, is deep within the inner depths, filling all space of our being. But the ignorant man knows it not; he is like a musk deer who has the musk within him, but runs to seek it without, driven by its sweet odor in all directions.

Realization of Nām is a gift (*dat*) of God, and not the result of meritorious deeds. How could conditional deeds bring union with the Unconditioned Being? It cannot be the result of them. As a little child crawling on his knees toward his mother makes the mother to get up with joy to take him into her loving arms, so does God through His mercy and grace advance to welcome a struggling soul into His everlasting embrace of love and compassion. He comes not to God through toil, nor through service, though both are needed in the growth of his being; he comes to Him when least expected by him. By His grace He joins His dearly beloved and His lover to His ever-loving blessed bosom. "All the adjustments of mind which contribute to the attainment of harmony and balance are very largely automatic and unconscious, even when self-consciousness and introspection are highly developed" is very keenly observed by the modern psychologist.

It does not mean that one should give up efforts. Efforts he must make, then realization is by His grace. Grace is the power that pulls the devotee to his God. Through the qualities (*gunas*) and meritorious conduct, the soul attracts the lover of souls. The utter nothingness of man's efforts and the all-compassionateness of His bounties are worth noticing and knowing.

After fully grasping and understanding the meaning (*gurumat*) of divine instruction in Truth, one must be ready to give up his own human way of life and living (*man-mat*) and fully incorporate the way of truth and *guru* until he is an embodiment of it in himself and knows it by having become it. This will further purify his nature and render him fit to receive grace. *Jāp* and *simran*, daily singing of His praise and mentally dwelling on His attributes, will further instill into his mind the beauty and grandeur of His Holy Nām. *Jāp* reading and repeating the holy scriptures and His praise are essential to saturate his mentality, until his whole attitude is God-minded (*guru-mukh*) and he deeply desires the blessed life.

As long as he has egoism (*houmen*), that long will he be in pains and pleasures alternately. His happiness, being rooted in the senses, will not be stable. Where egoism (*houmen*) is, Nām cannot make its home. Egoism and Nām are incompatible. True selfless service which elevates is not in egoism. Through the fulfillment of God's law and grace, egoism (*houmen*) is erased and effaced; it is the big cloud which hides the inner sun. There is no devotion in egoism, and hence the law cannot be fulfilled. Egoism binds the *jiva* to bondage. By meeting *sat-guru*, egoism disappears for good.

No sooner does man begin to work with the law of God, in thought, word, and deed, than the power and spirit of the law begins to grow upon him and changes him for the better. He is dyed with its spirit. It is the bounden duty of the disciple to follow faithfully the laws of life shown by his *guru*. He must be ready like a soldier, who is ever attentive to the carrying out of the commands of his general. Works and deeds which do not develop and transform man's character for the better are fruitless and useless expenditures of his energies.

Meditation on Nām and being pervaded by Nām are two different states. Selfishness (*khudi*) must be extirpated; then mind and body automatically become hale and hearty and heart pure to see Him who is all-worshipful. Through mind or ego alone is man a limited personality. When it is synthesized through the *shabad*, the indwelling Word, he is a spirit-person and bound no more. *Maya* and personality and pairs of opposites, the realm of duality, go together; and man cannot help being miserable as long as his focus remains there and he is tied to mortality as if by a cord. As soon as unification of mind is brought about, misery ceases to dominate him.

After acquiring intellectual knowledge of one's self, one must learn to know God in that self or no staying ground will be found for that self in the world of change, and it will be still pulled by earthly tendencies. Knowledge of the supreme path (*param-pad*), straight and narrow and sharp like a razor's edge, must be acquired by walking on this inner path of ascension. Mere verbal knowledge of the self alone is insufficient and will not bring permanent peace and joy of living. The self must wholeheartedly develop love and devotion for the Nām and find His being and form in the Nām and thus be drawn to His lotus feet.

He who in his heart by direct experience with Him is convinced of His presence, his mind and body will immediately act accordingly; all doubts will disappear. He whose mind is melted into Nām will know Him in his heart. *Param-pad*, the way to God within one's own being, is known by the destruction of selfishness and absorption in the Nām. To destroy separateness or egoism, one must walk on the path as outlined and shown by the *guru* and exalt his qualities of character to glorify Him, to become worthier in His sight. These are the essentials for the knowledge of God.

Those who acknowledge the universe also from God see everything and every event occurring in it from God, of God, and by God. They do not want to run away from the world, considering it a trap, but rather they rejoice that the Creator in His creation and creatures is being glorified now and here. *Sat-guru*, the savior, has not taught his Sikhs to give up hearth and home, daily deeds and enterprises, but rather to fulfill all natural inclinations in such an uplifting way that they will elevate the human into the divine state. Each must use rightly the things of this world and all worldly relations to build values which will make this present life lovely and the next lovelier on account of it.

Each is to regard all possessions as if he were their custodian and use them for his self-elevation and his fellow man's genuine benefit. All is his, so each one must learn to lose all sense of possessions. Only that could be his which has been built up as a merit, a quality and an attribute in his nature and character, which no one can ever take away from him. *Jiva*, mind, and body are all His. Know all to be His, see Him in all, serve Him in all, by all means, in all things. Time of labor is no longer different from the time of prayer and silence to him who knows God.

Sweetness and bitterness, goodness and evil, are not mutually exclusive qualities, but the opposite directions—ideally the opposite poles—of a process in which there is continuous gradation, so that the two qualities interpenetrate in varying degrees. All men are, in varying degrees, good and evil. The truly and wholly good is the divine person within each and all.

How vast is the whole curve of progress which the soul has to cover from its first birth to its final liberation, and how tiny is the arc represented by a single lifetime? The personal self can only "survive" by ever fading and changing toward the universal. The soul passes through great transformations, moultings, and sloughings and many metamorphoses before it can be fit for companionship with the great Author of its being; yet He is always available to all souls at all stages of their growth and unfoldment. The need for a thing is its true measure; it is both the seed and the promise of its fulfillment.

God and the self of man cannot be confined in a thought or any series or system of thought. All thinking is defining, and the Definer eludes. A self is not its thoughts, not its manifestations and experiences, although these express it, these enrich it, these are through and by which it grows, develops, plays its role, builds its world; and yet the self is not these. From the standpoint of thought, self is a mystery impenetrable. One must learn to leave all thoughts behind in one's inner journey to self and God and enter a higher order of knowledge, which is direct and foolproof. Truth cannot exist apart from the knower, or goodness from the evaluator. All dependent and derived existence is immortal only through its conscious realization of its relation to God. Parts can be understood only when interpreted through their membership in the Whole Person, the *akal-purkh*, to whom they all belong.

Where there is no self-consciousness (*chetna*), there is no chain of cause and consequence binding the soul (*karma*), by itself alone (as in the case of animals, or in the case of liberated men who are God-conscious), as the law would be unable to bring fruition by its own powers unless backed by the will of God as the regulator of all powers, of all beings, and all laws. God neither obeys laws of truth and goodness, nor reckons with them; but God, being perfection, goodness incarnate, in His personality expresses them. God, source and ground of the universe and all creatures, is free. He is determined, led, and compelled by nothing but Himself.

Man's perfection comes through the building of Godlike qualities in his character and working with the will and way of his Creator and Begettor. Being absorbed in His Holy Nām and anchored in it brings about the destruction of all *karmas* and liberation of his personal self from the bondage of *maya* and egoism. Modern thinkers admit that man's form is evolved through evolutionary processes and is connected with what has gone before it and carries the possibilities of what is yet to come after it. But nowhere do they admit an evolving personal, persistent self which, as it builds better qualities, enters into better vehicles of expression and equipment. As there is a unity, continuity, and identity of the self, as the self evolves, so evolve its means of contact with the world. Something permanently drastic and bitter always remains at the bottom of the individual's cup of life until the power of God's Word that put him in evolution pulls him up back to his unity with his Maker and lover, through the grace of *sant-satguru*, the living liberated divine way-shower and redeemer.

Creation (*rachna*) is not beginningless or endless (*anadi*). It has a beginning and ending in God, who remains untouched by either of the processes. *Maya*, *moha*, *bharam* are not the cause of creation, but they all come into being by His powers of the Holy Nām. He is seen by the pure in heart as working through and manifesting Himself in all beings and through all events. He is the only ever-awake and all-knowing being in the universe. The separating power of His Holy Nām that puts all beings into embodied existences and limitations is called *vijog*, and the uniting power that bring all beings back to His fatherly bosom is *sanjog*. They belong to Him. All the world's works are done by these two powers of the Living God working and through His living worlds.

God judges men not only according to their deeds and sense of perfect justice. He is the ever-compassionate (*dayal purkh*) and forgiving Father who brings all the strayed souls to His path of righteousness and grace. What is His knowledge? He is formless; His being cannot be the object of human thought. To be fully sure of His presence and possessed of His powers and to be guided by His will is to become absorbed and anchored in His Nām. His Nām and form are one and inseparable. This knowledge is gnosis, or *gayan*.

There is no need to hate others, for others are not the cause of our miseries. The root of miseries is within us. Cutting this root of misery from within without and transforming our nature and character, reading of scriptures and books, is useless. So long as mind is not "slain," real joy will remain an illusion. Merely sharpening one's *buddhi* or intellect does not bring peace, because all deeds are done by our nature (*subhava*) and not by our intelligence, and so long as *subhava* or character is not changed for the better, our mind will use its keen intellect for selfish and sinful advantages. By fulfilling *guru's* will, mind is gradually slain. As the inner light shines, all darkness will disappear, and lotuses will unfold upward and the light of the soul will blend with the light of the Lord and the twain shall be one.

When all the stains of mind are washed away, mind becomes luminous and is easily absorbed in the Nām, and being absorbed we become undifferentiated in Him. He is us, we are He, and this is arriving at one's own home (*nijdham*), home with the Father. This is *param-pad*, the supreme path and goal. Blessed is he whose only capital support and sustenance is His Holy Nām.

Where lust, anger, greed, passion, and egoism abide in the heart, there life is full of the world's fevers and feverish pursuits. Sickness, misery, and fear haunt the inner abode, and living is a "nightmare." With the advent of His Holy Nām they disappear and the entire being becomes healed and wholed once again. Holy Nām is the medicine of all medicines. He who possesses it in his heart soon finds out he cannot be sick again, even in dreams. This panacea for all human woes is in the heart of each and all; *guru* only shows the way to its recovery and possession.

Hands, feet, or the body, when dirty, are washed with water to clean them. When clothes are polluted by dirt, soap and water will make them clean. When intellect, mind, and heart are blackened by sin, Holy Nām will render them virgin, pure, and immaculate again. It is so and verifiable. *Maya*, by His will commanded, throws obstacles, hurdles, and hindrances in the way of all for their growth and elevation; but he who is fused and synthesized in His Nām becomes free from its trammels and is its lord and master now. Whether *jiva*, the self of man, is birthless (*anad*) or deathless and is caught in the web of *maya*, or whether God Himself puts ignorance in his nature to lead him astray—be it as it may, there is no release and transformation except through Nām.

To destroy the sense of separateness (*houmen*) and become one with the indwelling (*jot*) living light is the main objective placed before every aspirant of life divine by the *guru*. God is realized through the grace of the *guru* after wanderings of many births and deaths, comings and goings, and experiences on all levels of consciousness. When the *jiva*—the self—arrives at that stage of his soul-unfoldment where he hungers and thirsts for life eternal and the stable state of the spirit that nothing can shake from without, then *sat-guru* comes to lead him to his Lord within. *Sat-guru* is most generous; there is no generosity like his. Without *shabad*, Nām is never found. Through *sat-guru*'s grace it pervades the Sikh's mind. *Guru* grants him the light of gnosis (*gayan*) and his lamp is lit, his true eyes are opened. This inner light destroys all darkness within and without; mind with mind is joined, duality disappears, and man finds entrance into His realm of glory.

Nine doors are closed, so in and through them mind will not wander out, and through the tenth portal (*daswan dwar*) it enters within. Mind mingling with mind becomes single and unified, and in this state soundless sound (*anahad shabad*) is ringing day and night its song of life, and through the instructions of the gracious *guru* it is inwardly heard by the astral ears, and this music divine transfigures the soul. Without *guru*, this inner path is never found. Let none entertain any whims about it; it is invariably true. Man is ruled by his innate nature (*subhava*) and not by his intellectual knowledge (*vichar*). Such knowledge can be used to ameliorate and improve upon his nature by constant endeavor, but the transformation of his being will be accomplished by His Nām. Man's knowledge (*vichar*) cannot exceed its experience, and cannot go any further. In the circumstances in which human mind lives, it is affected by its environments. It becomes exactly like its surroundings; it cannot rise higher than its already established lines of movements or ruts will permit.

Before the advent of the Sikh *gurus*, it was believed that when darkness grew denser in the hearts and minds of men and virtue was eclipsed, then God Himself came in the form of an avatar to lead mankind by showing it the way back to Himself. But our Sikh *sat-gurus* say, "God is never born (*ajoni*). Father lacks nothing, is fullness in Himself; it is the *jivas* that are born, the perfected persons. On such occasions *sat-gurus* manifest themselves. *Guru* is used by the saviors in the sense of an avatar. These grand beings are sent by Him from above to manifest His truths by example and precept both, and they claim they are sent by Him and are fully conscious of their relations with Him, and at will can enter His divine state within. All embodied *gurus* (*deh-dhari*) of today have taken instructions from someone in the flesh, but *sat-guru* is born with the fullest knowledge. Our great *sat-guru*, Nanak Dev Ji, had no human *guru* to teach him. The great ones are sent by God through His grace; blessed by the fullness of His realization they come to earth. They alone should be called and considered *gurus*. *Guru* must be in complete realization of oneness with God or he cannot unite others to Him. Such a *sat-guru* takes no fee for his knowledge; he gives his all without the hope of reward through mercy, love, and compassion. Just as a mother bestows her heart's devotion and love on her children and nourishes them in many ways and protects them, so does the *sat-guru* love his Sikhs and devotees. His very sight cheers the hearts of his Sikhs, and their virtues are quickened by His touch and nearness. He joins his Sikhs to God by putting them on the path whereby they can know Him within themselves and by themselves. Without *guru*, *sahaja* state is not entered into and realized.

Walking in the footsteps of the true *guru* brings change. Man becomes what he lives. Inner life is metamorphosed, and he attains to Nām. Otherwise deeds done selfishly chain the soul further to earth and earthiness. As without the *guru*—the guide—the way of the Word is not found, so without association with the lofty-minded beings (*sat-sang*) it is impossible to walk on that way. Association with the lofty and meeting of morally minded men is included in every Sikh's daily prayers—*sadh da sang* and *gur mukh da mel*. He thus washes his old stains from his soul and builds new qualities that reinforce life.

Where *shabda* is radiated, discussed, and discoursed upon, there is congregation of the elect (*sat-sang*). The presence of *sat-guru* is the highest association, where truth is backed by love in example and by precepts. There is the association (*sat-sang*) that makes one ascend out of the *mayavic* environments into the moral and spiritual states. Saints—the *sat-gurus*—are the form of the Lord. Their sight makes life's harvest most fruitful. Their worship confers immutability, and one is released from comings and goings, and safely crosses the ocean of birth and death (*bhava sagar*).

Glossary

Agam The absolute and eternal being.

Aqua nostra His Holy Nām, which dissolves everything effete and renders the soul pure.

Akal purkh The ever-enduring being, the perfect, eternal being.

Amrita The nectar of immortality.

Anahat-shabad The soundless sound.

Avatar (mahatma) Completion of the individual.

Bhagats Devotees.

Bhava sagar When man is released from comings and goings and safely crosses the ocean of birth and death.

Binda The seat of the third eye.

Chaitan Self-conscious.

Chautha-pad A state in which man is neither conscious of the subjective nor conscious of the objective sides of life.

Chetna Where there is no self-consciousness.

Darshan To view and be in the company of a saint.

Daswan dwar The tenth portal. Nine portals are of physical nature; the tenth leads to God.

Dayal-purkh The ever-beneficent being in the Sunna region. Benevolent aspect of God.

Ganga Pure stream of God.

Gagan-mandal The galaxy of the inner sun.

Guru mantra Holy names.

Holy Nām The Word of God.

Houmen Original ignorance.

Jāpā Mental repetition of the Lord's name or a sacred formula given by a spiritual teacher.

Jarh Unconscious of its existence.

Jivan muktas The living liberated.

Jiva The superficial or apparent man.

Jot-narinjan Divine light.

Karma The principal of causation. The thoughts we habitually think, our mental states, our states of consciousness (levels of soul-awareness), and the actions we perform determine our experiences.

Karta-purkh The producing cause of the universe.

Khudi Selfishness.

Lal rung A glorious color; its dye ennobles ignoble substances.

Lamias Fairies or beguiling sirens who appear in the unconscious or subconscious.

Maya An illusion of mind.

Maya-moha Love of the world.

Mumta Love for passing things and thirst for things.

Nada The soundless sound.

Nām In the Nām, the Lord-God, the formless, assumes form, the nameless a name, and the infinite is definite; man is God, and God is man. Nām is called by many names in many countries and religions. (A) Christians: Verbum; Living Word; Divine Christos (B) Buddhists: Avalokiteswara (C) Pratyagatma (D) Pranva. Nām is the All Generator, the All Prayer and Purifier, Father and Lengthener of Life.

Nām de poh Tincture of the Holy Nām.

Nām khumari Divine wine.

Param-pad The way to God within one's own being by the destruction of selfishness and absorption in the Nām.

Prem Love divine.

Punch-shabad Five holy names.

Rajasic The principle of restlessness or activity of nature.

Sadh-sangat The company of lofty spirits.

Sahaja state Fulfillment, wholeness, complete realization of existence. The superconscious.

Sant-mat Science of spirituality.

Sat-guru Supreme teacher with absolute knowledge of the divine (God).

Sat-sang Association with the elect of mankind.

Sattvic Principal of light, harmony and balance.

Shabad The way of the Word.

Sushupati Deep sleep state, where there is no ego.

Shesh naga Monsters in the subconscious and the unconscious.

Simran of Nām Meditation on the Holy Name.

Subhava Disposition; way; own peculiar soul-nature and character.

Surt-shabad The repository of truth, life, light and love.

Tamasic That which is governed by a force of passion and activity.

Trikuti Home of universal mind; origin of all perishable minds.

Tirthas Center of creative transformation where the process of purification takes place.

Vichar Man's intellectual knowledge.